Library of
Davidson College

Foreign Investment Evaluation Practices of U.S. Multinational Corporations

Research for Business Decisions, No. 40

Gunter Dufey, Series Editor
Professor of International Business and Finance
The University of Michigan

Other Titles in This Series

No. 31 Pooled Data for Financial Markets Terry E. Dielman

No. 32 Capital Adequacy Requirements and Bank Holding Companies Itzhak Swary

No. 33 Commercial Banking and Holding Company Acquisitions: New Dimensions in Theory, Evaluation and Practice Larry A. Frieder

No. 34 Experience Effects in International Investment and Technology Transfer William H. Davidson

No. 35 Sales Training: An Analysis of Field Sales Techniques Alan J. Dubinsky

No. 36 An Income Tax Planning Model for Small Businesses David H. Butler

No. 37 Financial Forecasting in Banking: Methods and Applications Gary A. Giroux and Peter S. Rose

No. 38 The Prediction of Corporate Earnings Michael F. van Breda

No. 39 Common Stock Selection: An Analysis of Benjamin Graham's "Intelligent Investor" Henry Robert Oppenheimer

Foreign Investment Evaluation Practices of U.S. Multinational Corporations

by
Marie Wicks Kelly

UMI RESEARCH PRESS

Copyright © 1981, 1980
Marie Wicks Kelly
All rights reserved

Produced and distributed by
UMI Research Press
an imprint of
University Microfilms International
Ann Arbor, Michigan 48106

A revision of the author's thesis,
Pennsylvania State University, 1980

Library of Congress Cataloging in Publication Data

Kelly, Marie Wicks.
 Foreign investment evaluation practices of U.S. multinational corporations.

 (Research for business decisions ; no. 40)
 Revision of thesis, Pennsylvania State University, 1980.
 Bibliography: p.
 Includes index.
 1. Investments, Foreign–Evaluation. 2. Investments, American–Evaluation. 3. International business enterprises –Finance. 4. Corporations, American–Finance. I. Title. II. Series.
 HG4538.K43 1981   332.6'7314   81-4714
 ISBN 0-8357-1183-8

Contents

Acknowledgments	vii
Introduction	1

Chapter

1 Definitions and Issues of MNCs — 5
   Foreign Direct Investment — 5
   Multinational Corporations — 5
   The Controversial MNCs — 6
   Empirical Evaluations of Controversies
     Surrounding MNCs — 10

2 Investment Decisions of the MNC:
   Aggregate Approach — 17
   Positive Theories of Foreign Direct Investment — 17
   Empirical Tests of Positive Theories — 22

3 Investment Decisions of the MNC: Firm Approach — 27
   Normative Theories of Firm International
     Investment Decisions — 27
   Political Risk — 30
   Foreign Exchange Risk — 33
   Positive Theories of Firm International Investment
     Decisions — 34

4 Traditional Versus Behavioral Theory of Firm
   Decisions — 35

5 Methodology — 41
   Overview — 41
   Sample Selection — 42
   Survey and Field Study Research — 44
   The Questionnaire — 49
   The Field Study — 55

vi Contents

    Anticipated Results   59
    Analysis of Results   62
    Summary   64

6 Results   67
    Overview   67
    Characteristics of Responding Firms   68
    Documentation of Foreign Investment
      Evaluation Practices   71
    Relationships of Demographic and Organizational Variables
      to Foreign Investment Evaluation Practices   102
    The Field Study   144

7 Summary and Conclusions   159
    Summary of Study Purpose, Methodology, and
      Background   159
    Comparison of Prior and Present Studies   161
    Comparison of Anticipated and Actual Results of
      Present Study   169
    Summary of Comparisons   176
    Future Research   177

Appendix A. Companies Included in Present Survey and
Harvard Multinational Enterprise Study   179

Appendix B. Cover Letter and Questionnaire Used in
Present Survey Research   191

Appendix C. Questions Covered in Field Survey   215

Notes   219

Bibliography   221

Index   231

Acknowledgments

I wish to express my sincere appreciation to Professor George C. Philippatos, without whose guidance and insight this study would not have been possible. I am grateful to Professor J. Russ Ezzell, Professor John D. Daniels, and Dr. Willard E. Witte for their comments and suggestions. I would like to thank Professor James C. McDavid for his assistance with the quantitative aspects of this research.

This work could not have been completed without the help of Miss Crystal Stover, whose assistance in preparing and mailing the questionnaire was greatly appreciated. A very special thanks is extended to Ms. Mary Frank, Mr. Robert Stevenson, and Mrs. Karen Steinde for their considerable guidance and contribution.

I am very grateful to the Richard D. Irwin Company for selecting me as a recipient of an award enabling me to devote my full attention and energies to my research.

Special and heartfelt thanks go to Jim Kelly, without whose cheerful encouragement and patience this study would not have been possible.

Introduction

Since the mid-1950s the multinational corporation (MNC) has increasingly become one of the dominant vehicles for the international exchange of resources, skills, knowledge, services, and finished goods. According to a United Nations report,

> The value added of all multinational corporations, estimated roughly at $500 billion in 1971 was about one-fifth of world gross national product. Sales of foreign affiliates of multinational corporations has surpassed trade as the main vehicle of the international economic exchange. (*Multinational Corporations in World Development,* 1973, pp. 13-14)

This powerful and growing economic force has been the center of considerable controversy regarding its impact on the economic, social, and political well-being of its home base as well as the countries in which it invests.

On one side of the controversy are those who say that with its technological and managerial expertise, coupled with its global perspective, the MNC is the "engine for world development, the great leveler [between rich and poor nations], [the instrument for the] use of world resources with a maximum of efficiency and a minimum of waste... on a global scale"(Barnet and Müller, 1974, pp. 14, 20). Those who take this point of view argue that in the search for global-profit maximization, the MNC allocates resources optimally worldwide to the benefit of its home country and the countries receiving its investment as well.

However, there are numerous groups who take issue with this view of the MNC. To name but a few: organized labor in the United States, who argues that the MNC invests overseas in order to take advantage of cheaper labor and thus exports U.S. jobs; local businesses in the recipient country who face takeovers or severe competition from oligopolistically powerful MNCs; home-country government authorities who see the flexibility of the MNC moving it increasingly outside of their control; recipient country governments who feel a loss of national sovereignty because of their dependence on the MNC for the technology, capital, and skills necessary for development. Each of these groups argues that the MNC generates costs which far outweigh the benefits of allocative efficiency.

Such fundamental disagreements about the role of the MNC in the world economy have generated a wealth of studies falling into four broad categories:

(1) positive theories of foreign direct investment at the aggregate level (Polk, Meister, and Veit, 1966; Aliber, 1970; Servan-Schreiber, 1968; Horst, 1972; Ray, 1977; Boatwright and Renton, 1975; Caves, 1974; Vernon, 1966; Scaperlanda and Mauer, 1969; Brems, 1970) and their empirical tests; (2) theoretical and empirical research into the impact of foreign direct investment on the home and host economies (Hymer, 1960; Goldfinger, 1971; Hufbauer and Adler, 1968; Behrman, 1968; Lindert, 1971; Stevens, 1976; Vernon, 1973; Stobaugh, 1969; Reddaway, 1968; Safarian, 1973; Johnson, 1970; Gray and Makinen, 1967; Adler and Stevens, 1974); (3) normative theories of foreign direct investment at the firm level (Rodriquez and Carter, 1976; Eiteman and Stonehill, 1973; Dymsza, 1972; Zenoff and Zwick, 1969; Richardson, 1971; Stonehill and Nathanson, 1968; Stobaugh, 1969; Rugman, 1975; Gaddis, 1966; Treuherz, 1968); and (4) positive analysis of the foreign investment decision at the firm level (Aharoni, 1966; Robbins and Stobaugh, 1973; Stonehill and Nathanson, 1968; Kim, 1976; Piper, 1971; Kossack, 1977; Morris, 1968).

In the first category, six major positive theories have been advanced: (1) differential interest rates (traditional); (2) growth of the firm (Polk, Meister, and Veit, 1966); (3) abilities and competitive advantage (Hymer, 1960); (4) R&D capability in the product life cycle (Vernon, 1966); (5) capital intensity under differential income valuation (Aliber, 1970); and (6) management superiority (Servan-Schreiber, 1968). Unfortunately, empirical evaluations of these theories have not produced general agreement on the superiority of any one explanation.

In the second category, the impact of MNCs on the home and host economies is still open to debate. Whether the MNC has a beneficial effect in terms of employment, economic growth, competition, and the balance of payments critically depends on assumptions made about the motives for foreign direct investment (defensive versus aggressive) and what would have occurred in the absence of overseas commitments by the MNC.

Normative theories of foreign direct investment, the third category, parallel the first two areas in the lack of agreement between prominent theories. Application of traditional domestic capital-budgeting approaches to the more complex international environment has left unanswered such issues as: Whose cash flows, parent or subsidiary, should be used in investment evaluation? Whose cost of capital is relevant for discounted cash flow analysis? How should the additional risks in international business, e.g., foreign exchange and political risk, be incorporated?

Several steps have been taken toward answering these questions as well as some of the issues in the first two categories by the positive analysis of the international investment decision at the firm level. One of the earliest and most comprehensive of these studies was by Aharoni who analyzed the foreign investment decision from a behavioral theory approach.

As G.P.E. Clarkson states, "whether one desires to construct a positive theory or to compare the results of a normative theory with existing procedures, a knowledge of actual behavior is a prerequisite"(Clarkson, 1962, pp. 1-2). Such a prerequisite has only begun to be fulfilled by the research to date. This study seeks to expand the understanding of the international investment decision process by focusing on actual behavior of multinational companies. Thus, the goals of the research are to:

1. Document the international investment motives and evaluation practices used by a sample of U.S.-based manufacturing MNCs.
2. Discover the significant variables and relationships between variables in the international investment decision process of MNCs.
3. Test broad hypotheses on international investment decision-making drawn from the traditional and the behavioral theory frameworks.

A questionnaire in conjunction with an in-depth field study is the methodology used to meet these objectives.

The focus of the research is positive at the firm level. The results should provide important information for:

1. explaining corporate foreign investment behavior and its economic impact;
2. formulating policies to influence foreign investment flows; and
3. examining the explanatory value of different theories of foreign investment.

The remainder of this study expands upon the issues and details of the research mentioned above. Chapter 1 provides definitions and an enumeration of the central controversies surrounding the MNC. Chapters 2 and 3 present a review of the foreign direct-investment research at the aggregate and firm levels, respectively. Chapter 4 contains a description of the traditional and the behavioral theories of the firm (Cyert and March, 1962) and their applications to international investment decisions. Chapter 5 outlines the methodology of this research, while Chapter 6 details the results. Chapter 7 is reserved for summary remarks.

1
Definitions and Issues of MNCs

Foreign Direct Investment

Since the subject of this research is the overseas direct-investment decisions of U.S. manufacturing multinational corporations, it is important to clarify what foreign direct investment is, what companies are multinationals, and what the major issues surrounding these corporations are. Foreign direct investment is more limited in scope than international or foreign investment (Daniels, Ogram, and Radebaugh, 1976, pp. 33-34). The latter concept encompasses the ownership of both long-term and short-term assets in one country by individuals or organizations of another country and, as such, includes both portfolio and direct investment. The distinguishing feature of direct investment is that the foreign investor acquires sufficient interest to have control of the overseas operation. Although the size of an interest necessary for control depends on the degree of dispersion of a company's stock, the conventional measure used in government and private studies is that a minimum ownership of 10-25 percent of the voting stock of a foreign operation constitutes a direct investment.[1] The 25 percent minimum criterion is the standard used in this research in the belief that the stock of a foreign company is generally less widely held than in the United States so that the higher minimum is a better indicator of control.

Multinational Corporations

Turning to the definition of a multinational corporation, one of the earliest uses of the term was by D.E. Lilienthal, who meant a "company with industrial or commercial operations abroad which directly involve managerial responsibility" (1960, p. 2).[2] Central to his definition was the idea that a multinational company should have more than just a financial stake or sales and distribution operation abroad. The concept was expanded by Vernon, who considered the key feature of a multinational corporation to be power characterized by large size, geographic spread, flexibility, and common resources and strategy (1971, p. 4). Various other rules of thumb for defining the multinational corporation include number of countries of foreign operations, ownership from many countries, nationality of top management, and organizational structure.

These methods of defining the multinational are what Aharoni has called structural approaches. He details several other ways to classify multinationals, such as performance yardsticks, behavioral characteristics, and his suggested combined approach. Performance yardsticks include relative and absolute measures of overseas sales, assets, earnings, and employees. Behavioral characteristics focus on corporate management's orientation, i.e., on the ability to think globally, to limit affiliation with any one country as home, and to view the entire world as a market.

According to Aharoni, each of the approaches has limitations. Behavioral characteristics are difficult to operationalize while performance yardsticks suffer from definitional problems, e.g., in selecting the currency for measurement, in setting a level of significance, etc. Structural approaches include too many types of operations in a single term. He suggests three main classifications:

> (1) the worldwide company—registered in several countries and doing business in these countries; (2) a multinational cluster—a group of corporations, each created in the country of operation, but all controlled by one headquarter; (3) a multinational corporation—a corporation which controls a multinational cluster. (Aharoni, 1971, p. 27)

He further suggests that the multinational cluster should include companies in at least six countries.

This approach parallels that used by Vernon (1971) and Robbins and Stobaugh (1973) in the Harvard Multinational Enterprise Project. For the sake of comparability of results, this definition will be used in the present study as well. To review, a foreign direct investment is the acquisition by a company of one country of at least 25 percent of the voting stock of a company in a second country. A multinational corporation is the parent company controlling operations in at least six countries.

The Controversial MNCs

Two key characteristics follow from the definition of the MNC—it operates across national boundaries, and final control of these operations rests with a foreign parent. These characteristics give rise to much of the controversy concerning the economic, social/cultural, and political impact of the MNC. Because the MNC transfers resources across national boundaries, it affects the economic environment of each country in which it operates via employment, income distribution, the balance of payments, the rate of economic development, and competition. Second, the MNC's geographic dispersion implies a degree of flexibility unapproachable by domestic companies. That, coupled with the loss of control over decisions inherent in parent-subsidiary relations, is a source of concern for home- and host-country governments, labor unions, and competitors.

In this research the economic impacts of multinational operations are of prime concern and will be discussed in detail in the remainder of this chapter. For completeness, a brief review will also be presented of the controversies surrounding the MNC's impact on the social/cultural and political environments of the countries in which it operates.

Turning first to employment, one of the sharpest critics of the MNC is organized labor in the United States. Its position is that in seeking to maximize profits worldwide, MNCs exploit cheap labor overseas, thus exporting U.S jobs. Union spokesmen state that MNC direct investment substitutes for domestic investment and is aggressive in nature aimed at labor-cost minimization. One study sponsored by U.S. labor groups attributes 500,000 jobs lost from 1966-1969 to foreign investment activities of U.S. MNCs (Goldfinger, 1971). In addition, they see the flexibility of MNC operations as a major deterrent to the transnational spread of organized-labor activities. The ability to switch operations to a sister subsidiary in the event of a strike or work slowdown limits the effectiveness of such actions. Thus, U.S. labor views the MNC as a threat to its existence and growth.

The MNCs' counterargument to labor's claims is that direct investment tends to be defensive in nature, i.e., that they invest overseas to save a market from being lost. As such, the jobs lost would have been lost in any case and so cannot be attributed to the advent of overseas operations. They also claim to create domestic jobs in order to service their foreign operations, e.g., employment in the manufacturing of component and replacement parts, headquarters staff positions, etc. (Hawkins, 1972).

The MNCs also claim to have a favorable employment impact in the countries in which they invest. They employ idle workers, create jobs in ancillary industries, improve wages, provide training, and develop a local managerial cadre. Critics disagree, saying that the MNC does very little training, uses mostly home-country managers in local operations, monopolizes the limited skilled labor available in many host countries, and in turn raises wages exorbitantly, but only for a few workers.

The wage issues relate directly to the impact MNCs have on income distribution in home and host countries. In traditional theory, the efficient allocation of resources by the MNC should result in a leveling of incomes worldwide. However, some have argued that rather than supplying the poorer regions of the world with resources that they need, MNCs have exploited the scarce resources already there. In this way, MNCs are said to have widened the gap between rich and poor nations (Barnet and Müller, 1974, pp. 148-84). In addition, as mentioned above, MNCs may exacerbate the problem of unequal income distribution within less developed host countries by inflating the wages of a few skilled workers.

Another controversy almost as heated as the job issue is the impact that MNCs have on home- and host-country balance of payments. The MNC claims to have a potentially positive impact on both countries' balance of payments. For the donor country, the initial foreign direct-investment outflow should be more than offset by future dividends, royalties, and fees. In addition, the overseas investment results in increased exports, e.g., replacement and component parts, consumer goods as incomes rise overseas, etc. This viewpoint assumes that foreign direct investment does little export displacement. Dissenters claim the opposite, i.e., U.S. exports and direct investment are substitutes [see Hufbauer and Adler (1968), Behrman (1968), Hawkins (1972), Horst (1976), and Adler and Stevens (1974) for a more detailed description].

For the host country an initial-capital inflow from direct investment has a positive balance-of-payments effect. In addition, local production may substitute for former imports, and goods may be produced for export, resulting in a further balance-of-payments improvement. However, it is also possible that imports into the host may increase more than exports if, for example, the MNC produces for a local market only and uses imported supplies or if, as found by Lall (1973), MNCs export less and at lower prices than local firms. MNC transfer pricing may also negatively affect the balance of payments if companies overprice exports to their affiliates and underprice exports from affiliates as research by Vaistos (1972) indicates. Finally, the future flows back to the investing parent have a negative balance-of-payments effect (Barnet and Müller, 1974).

As this brief description indicates, the balance-of-payments impacts of multinational operations depend critically on the time span considered, the motives for direct investment, and the assumptions made about what would have resulted in the absence of direct investment. A complete review of this issue is reserved for Chapter 2.

The fourth controversy surrounding the MNC because of its operations across borders is its impact on economic development. One of the keys to economic development is the distillation and utilization of technology. U.S.-based MNCs have been the wellspring of innovation, and the comparative strength of the U.S. economy vis-à-vis the rest of the world has been in high-technology products (Vernon, 1971). Less developed countries view the acquisition of technology as a basis for industrialization. As the MNC transfers technology between countries via its international operations, it is open to criticism from both sides. Critics at home contend that the MNC is transferring away the comparative advantage of the United States with disastrous economic implications. Host countries contend that in order to spread costs and increase profits MNCs transfer old technology; that due to the oligopsony market the price of technology is too high; that the technology is inappropriate, i.e., too capital-intensive for their needs; and that research is centralized at home, keeping them forever dependent on the MNC for new technology (Barnet and Müller, 1974). As host countries are growing more knowledgeable and powerful in their dealings with MNCs, the technology transfer issues will continue to be an area of dissension.

The competitive effect of multinational companies remains an important issue as well. One view of the MNC asserts that the growth of foreign operations increases competition locally, where a subsidiary is started, as well as worldwide. Increased competition should have the beneficial effects of classical economics, e.g., more efficient allocation of resources, lower prices, greater consumer choice, etc. But others argue to the contrary; that MNCs are large firms operating in imperfect markets (Hymer, 1970). Their investment decisions are made to maintain an oligopolistic balance worldwide or to exploit some monopolistic advantage. As such, direct investment may reduce competition, efficiency, and consumer choice. The tendency of many firms to enter a foreign market via acquisition of local companies lends some support to this view.

Turning to the social/cultural and political results of the cross-border operations of MNCs, the first is their impact on distinct national cultures. One view is that the MNC is improving the standard of living worldwide. However, others charge that the MNC forces a Westernization of the countries in which it operates through the products it offers, its advertising, its work codes, and standards (Barnet and Müller, 1974). The destruction of local culture and the creation of inappropriate wants is a prime area of conflict between the MNC and nation states.

But the critical issue for sovereign states is their loss of power to multinationals. This issue is important to both home and host countries. Home countries find that the flexibility of MNC operations allows these firms to circumvent domestic economic policies. For example, MNCs have been accused of avoiding taxation in the United States by manipulation of transfer prices within the corporate network. For developed host countries, similar problems exist.

But for the less developed host country a more important threat arises because of the foreign locus of decision-making in the MNC rather than from its flexibility per se. Although MNCs claim to be good corporate citizens of each country in which they operate, the final decisions come from corporate headquarters, i.e., outside the host country. Less developed hosts view this economic dependence as a direct threat to their national sovereignty.

Additionally, the parent company is ultimately responsible to the laws of the home country. As such, the MNC is seen as a tool for "economic imperialism." Thus, both home and host countries cite areas where the MNC is beyond their control. The extent to which the MNC "slips between the cracks" is still open to debate.

The MNC by definition mobilizes resources across national borders but retains ultimate decision-making in the parent country. Because of these characteristics, the MNC has generated considerable controversy about the impact of its operations. In an effort to resolve these issues, a voluminous amount of research has been conducted. A review of the main contribution to this research follows.

Empirical Evaluations of Controversies Surrounding MNCs

Of the numerous charges leveled against the MNC, two have been studied most extensively: the impact of foreign direct investment (FDI) on the balance of payments and the effect of overseas operations on employment. Because these two areas are of primary importance for policy development, they are the focus of this section.

One of the most complete analyses of the impacts of FDI was conducted by Hufbauer and Adler (1968). They sought to determine the impact of manufacturing direct investment on the U.S. balance of payments. As a measure of the balance-of-payments impact, they estimated the average recoupment period for an overseas investment. This measure, which parallels that used in an earlier study by Bell (1962), represents the number of years it takes for the return flow of interest payments, dividends, royalty fees, etc. to equal the initial outflow from a foreign investment. Using U.S. foreign manufacturing investment data from various parts of the world for the period 1950-1965, they found that the recoupment period was never less than 6.5 years, and in many cases return inflows did not equal the initial outflow in less than 20 years.

One of the most important contributions of the Hufbauer and Adler research was their analysis of the trade effects of foreign investment and, in particular, their emphasis on the export displacement impact of foreign investment. They theorized three situations related to export displacement which have been used extensively in subsequent research. The first, called the classical situation, hypothesized that sales of a foreign subsidiary of a multinational corporation did not supplant native firm sales but directly substituted for imports, i.e., direct investment added to capital formation abroad, and created a local supply substituting for exports from the United States. In this case, foreign investment and output increase, home investment and output decrease, and total world investment is unchanged. The second, called the reverse classical hypothesis, assumed that any increase in foreign subsidiary sales displaced only local firm sales and that imports were unaffected, i.e., direct investment had no local capital formation impact and exports from the United States remained intact. Again, total world investment is unchanged, as either local or third-country investment declines equal to home foreign investment. The third case, called the anticlassical, assumed that foreign subsidiary sales did not displace local productions and left imports unchanged. In this case, overseas investment and output increases while home-country investment and output is unchanged, so world investment increases as well.

Hufbauer and Adler calculated recoupment periods for investments in various parts of the world under each of the three cases. Table 1 shows their estimated recoupment periods and the cumulative effect of a direct investment after 20 years. In many cases, the recoupment periods are long, and in several cases the net effect is still negative after 20 years. It is important that the estimated impact of a foreign investment on the home country's balance of payments varies significantly depending on the export displacement assumptions employed.

In reviewing their work, Behrman (1968) contended that Hufbauer and Adler had been too pessimistic in their formulation of the trade-feedback effects of direct investment. Based on his case studies of 53 companies, he disputed as too conservative the following assumptions made by Hufbauer and Adler:

1. They assumed that either the United States or a foreigner invested, not both.
2. They blamed the loss of U.S. exports on direct investment, when the export loss actually resulted from foreign government restrictions precluding exports.
3. They discounted the sale of capital equipment overseas, assuming that it would have occurred with or without direct investment.
4. They gave little credit to the export expansion of supplies and materials, and no credit for increased exports in anticipation of investment.

Behrman reformulated the Hufbauer and Adler model with more positive trade-effect assumptions. He postulated a case where home-country foreign investment is complemented by, rather than substituted for, local or third-country investment. His assumptions are those of Hufbauer and Adler's reverse classical scenario but with complementary investment by local or third-country companies, i.e., foreign investment and foreign subsidiary sales represent a net addition to world investment and sales, while U.S. exports

Table 1

Impact of Manufacturing Foreign Investment on U.S. Balance of Payments[a]

| Trade Effect Assumption | Area of Investment ||||||||
| | Canada || Latin America || Europe || Rest of the World ||
	RP[b]	Cum. Effect[c]	RP	Cum. Effect	RP	Cum. Effect	RP	Cum. Effect
Classical Case	--	-14.2	--	-1.2	7.5	3.5	22.2	0.9
Reverse Classical Case	10.2	2.6	9.8	3.0	6.5	5.0	8.1	6.6
Anticlassical Case	--	-15.0	--	-1.8	10.8	2.3	--	-0.6

[a]Data for this table come from Hufbauer and Adler (1968).

[b]RP = recoupment period in number of years.

[c]Cum. Effect = cumulative impact of investment at 20 years in millions of U.S. dollars.

remain intact. Under these assumptions and using data for 1957-1965, Behrman found much shorter recoupment periods, e.g., two years for U.S. investment in Europe, one year for Canada, and one year for Latin America.

Behrman's results underscore the importance of the trade-effect assumptions in the estimation of the balance-of-payments impact of foreign investment.[3]

Many studies have addressed the controversy about the impact of multinational operations on the balance of payments, and with little consensus. The same holds true for the employment effects of direct investment.[4] Organized labor in the United States claimed a net job loss of 500,000 due to the international operations of multinational corporations from 1966-1969. Using Department of Labor data, they calculated that in 1966 about 1.8 million jobs would have been required to produce 74 percent of U.S. imports assumed competitive with U.S.-made products. By 1969, the comparable figure was 2.5 million workers, or an increase of 700,000 million "lost" jobs. From this was subtracted 200,000 jobs attributed to increased exports for a net loss of 500,000 jobs (*The Multinational Corporation: Studies on U.S. Foreign Investment*, 1973).

Labor's position has been summarized by Nathaniel Goldfinger:

> One of the underlying causes of the deterioration of the U.S. position in world trade is the operations of U.S.-based multinational companies, with far-flung foreign subsidiaries, patent and licensing arrangements with foreign companies, joint venture deals and other foreign arrangements. . . . The operations of U.S.-based multinationals have exported American technology, with the loss of U.S. production and employment, for the private advantage of the firm. They are a major factor in the rapid and substantial loss of U.S. production in such relatively sophisticated goods as radios, televisions, and other electrical products, as well as in shoes and apparel. . . . What may be rational decisions for . . . a U.S.-based multinational may spell disaster for large numbers of American workers, small business firms, and several entire communities. . . . A large and growing part of what is called U.S. exports and imports are now transactions within the structures of these multinational firms—between the U.S.-based company and its foreign subsidiaries. . . . U.S. trade patterns are thereby affected by the operations of the multinational—and the shape of many American industries and communities, as well. The U.S. government cannot much longer permit the private decisions of multinationals to determine the future of the American economy, without regulations. (Goldfinger, 1971, p. 19)

Multinational corporations have disputed this view and a number of studies have supported their position. Three are reviewed here. Taking a survey approach, the research firm Business International (1974) analyzed 133 companies whose foreign investments accounted for over half of U.S. foreign manufacturing investments. For the period 1960 to 1972, the sample group raised domestic employment by 48.8 percent and by 17.1 percent from 1966-1972. All U.S. manufacturing firms showed only 14.3 percent and 4.7 percent increases for the same period. Additionally, the survey found that job security appeared to be greater with heavy foreign investors than with domestic firms. Heavy foreign investors could maintain their profit margins and dividend ratios better during a U.S. recession than domestic companies and so resorted to less budget-cutting and fewer layoffs. As a final test, the sample firms were divided into quartiles based on their foreign intensity, and a strong correlation was discovered between foreign intensity and increase in U.S. employment.

Applying regression analysis to industry statistics for the period 1966-1970, Horst (1976) found similar results. He found that foreign direct investment showed no statistical causation for the pattern of U.S. exports and imports. Additionally, industries that exported more also produced more abroad. He concluded that while foreign manufacturing investment could displace U.S. production (decreasing jobs), nonmanufacturing investments created a market for U.S. goods (increasing jobs).

Research by Hawkins (1972) supported this view that foreign investment may have an asymmetrical effect on U.S. employment. Using data for 19 industries from 1963-1970, he compared the domestic economic performance of high- and low-foreign-intensity industries and found that:

1. Industries with high foreign investment intensity tended, on average, to have export surpluses. As the overall trade balance of the United States deteriorated substantially in the late 1960s, high foreign investment industries experienced less deterioration or greater improvement in their export-import position than did relatively low foreign investment industries.
2. The increase in the portion of U.S. production of goods which was exported in the late sixties was also positively related to the intensity of foreign direct investment by industry.
3. Average growth in U.S. employment proved to be higher, on average, in industries with high intensities of foreign investment than in those with low; a similar relationship was found for growth in U.S. production. (Hawkins, 1972, p.i)

Hawkins (1972) later found that the job loss that might have been attributable to displacement by manufacturers abroad occurred in job classes different than the job gains from increased exports due to foreign investment. He found that job losses were of the low-skill production type while job gains were skilled production, staff, and managerial opportunities. Thus, although the overall effect of MNC operations on employment may be positive, the effect on organized labor's constituency may be negative.

The employment and balance-of-payments controversies remain unresolved. In both cases, many of the arguments in support of MNC activities are based on the view that the MNC allocates resources optimally worldwide and thus benefits both home and host countries. Positive theories of foreign direct-investment behavior provide a starting point for understanding factors leading to foreign investments and so determine how resources are allocated. The following two chapters explore the positive research on foreign direct investment: first at the aggregate, and then at the firm level.

2
Investment Decisions of the MNC: Aggregate Approach

Inquiries into the behavior of multinationals in the aggregate fall into two groups. The first group has investigated the reasons why companies make foreign direct investments, seeking to develop positive theories of international capital flows. The second group has focused on the impact that such capital flows have on the home- and host-country economies, their main purpose being policy recommendations. These studies have concentrated primarily on the employment and balance-of-payments effects of multinational operations. They were presented in the previous chapter. A review of the main contributors in the first category follows.

Positive Theories of Foreign Direct Investment

There are six major positive theories of foreign direct investment at the aggregate level:[1] (1) differential interest rates (traditional); (2) growth of the firm (Polk, Meister, and Veit, 1966); (3) abilities and competitive advantages (Hymer, 1960); (4) R&D capability in the product life cycle (Vernon, 1966); (5) capital intensity under differential income valuation (Aliber, 1970); and (6) managerial superiority (Servan-Schreiber, 1968). Turning first to the differential interest rates theory, this approach uses a model of international trade theory to explain capital flows but deletes the traditional assumption of factor immobility. It assumes instead absent or impeded trade while retaining the assumptions of free information and perfect competition. In this formulation, capital moves internationally as long as the marginal product of capital is not equal between countries, the usual criterion of capital productivity being the interest rate, as formulated by Ohlin in his shift in emphasis to factor endowments in international trade theory. Thus, "interest rate differentials are the most important stimulus to foreign investment" (Ohlin, 1967).

This approach has several theoretical deficiencies as well as a general lack of support in empirical research. First, the introduction of information costs and the concept of risk makes the calculation of equal interest rates difficult. Observed variations in risk preference make actual interest rates unsuitable for predicting capital movements because investors with differing risk perceptions and information needs may be indifferent to a wide range of prevailing interest rates.

Second, trade in capital-intensive goods leads to equalization of interest rates even in the absence of international capital movements. Factors of production, e.g., capital, move when trade barriers exist and the existence of trade barriers makes the assumption of free competition suspect.

Finally, the differential interest rate theory does not explain the cross investment and equity investment to gain control typical of MNC investment activity. Nor does it explain the observed pattern of foreign investment which is concentrated in a few countries and industries.

Several empirical studies (Moose, 1968; Kotowitz, Sawyer, and Winder, 1968; Kwack, 1970; Prachowrsy, 1970) have found that actual interest-rate differentials between host and source countries are small, and that no significant relationship exists between foreign investment flows and interest rates. Using a questionnaire approach with an individual company focus, Polk, Meister, and Veit (1966) found similar results.

The second theory, the growth of the firm explanation of foreign direct investment, was advanced by Polk because of the responses to a questionnaire survey conducted by the National Industrial Conference Board in the mid-1960s (Polk, Meister, and Veit, 1966). The business community replied overwhelmingly that business investors seek markets. Firms are motivated to seek overseas opportunities by the potential for increasing market share, volume of sales, and earnings-to-sales ratios. Thus, foreign investment is seen as a response either to domestic obstacles to growth or to attactive overseas opportunities, e.g., strong overseas demand or the chance to obtain economies of scale abroad.

Although this theory has considerable empirical support in survey research, it has explanatory limitations. First, it focuses on companies' willingness to invest overseas but largely ignores their ability to do so, e.g., their profitability. Second, the theory does not explain the prevalence of direct investment versus foreign investment as a means for achieving growth objectives. The third limitation of this approach is its inability to explain withdrawal of investments once they have been made.

The next four approaches, those of Hymer, Vernon, Aliber, and Servan-Schreiber, seek to explain the competitive advantages of investing companies vis-à-vis local competitors. They emphasize why companies enter foreign markets through direct rather than portfolio investments.

The third positive theory, that proposed by Hymer (1960), takes the view, unlike traditional approaches, that "direct investment belongs more to the theory of industrial organization than to the theory of international capital movements." Hymer contends that for foreign direct investment to occur, the firm must earn a higher return overseas than a local firm. Merely to earn a higher return abroad than at home is not sufficient, because in that case capital would move through specialized capital markets, not via a MNC. In order to earn more than a local firm, the foreign firm must overcome the disadvantages of distance and foreignness, each of which is costly. Thus, to compete, the foreign firm must maintain some monopolistic advantage that local firms cannot obtain. This implies that in order for foreign direct investment to take place, there must be imperfections in the market for goods or factors, and these imperfections can result from some interference in competition by governments or firms.

Kindleberger catalogues the types of monopolistic advantages that lead to direct investment as follows (1969, p. 274):

1. departures from perfect competition in the goods markets, including product differentiation, special marketing skills, retail price maintenance, administered pricing.
2. departures from perfect competition in the factor markets, including the existence of patented technology, of discrimination in access to capital, of differences in skills of managers organized in firms rather than hired in competitive markets.
3. internal and external economies of scale, the latter being taken advantage of by vertical integration.
4. government limitation on output or entry.

Using these types of competitive advantages, Hymer considers exporting and licensing as alternatives to direct investment. He theorizes, for example, that a company will service foreign markets by exporting if the advantage decreases in the transfer, e.g., if the advantage is based on land. Similarly, the company would export if components cost more than finished goods to ship. The introduction of tariffs would stimulate foreign investment. The MNC would be expected to license if it has only part of the resources necessary for production.

Hymer's approach makes several important contributions to the theory of foreign investment. In addition to focusing attention on the types of monopolistic advantages that could lead to direct investment and the conditions under which foreign markets might be served via exports, licensing, or direct investment, he analyzes why companies desire to control assets overseas (as opposed to making portfolio investments). He suggests four reasons: (1) to protect failing portfolio investments; (2) to diversify operations; (3) to decrease international competition; and (4) to gain a full share of the returns from proprietary abilities. Hymer selects the last two as the most important reasons.

Despite these contributions, the Hymer theory has at least two limitations. He does not address the relative importance of various monopolistic abilities in explaining foreign investment patterns. Nor does he explain the nature and distribution of local barriers to equal competition. The next theory, Vernon's product life-cycle approach, addresses this issue.

During the Multinational Enterprise Project at Harvard, Vernon (1971) observed a recurring pattern of manufacturing investment abroad. U.S. companies typically generated new products first for the home market. These products reflected the demand and relative factor availability of the United States and so tended to be high-income, labor-saving innovations. When new products were introduced, they often exhibited a large degree of differentiation resulting in at least a temporary monopoly advantage for the manufacturer. As such, the location of production was controlled more by the necessity of being close to the market than the need for low-cost production sites. So the U.S. market was initially serviced from U.S. production.

As other economies, Europe in particular, recovered from the economic chaos of World War II, they began to exhibit characteristics of the U.S. economy, i.e., high incomes and a growing need for labor-saving technology. To fill this demand, U.S. companies began to service markets abroad through exports. But as products gained acceptance overseas, local producers were attracted to the market. Additionally, as the product matured, production processes became more standardized and buyers became more price responsive. These changes made the U.S. producers more sensitive to cost-oriented production locations. At this stage, threatened by the loss of markets serviced through exports, the U.S. company commenced production overseas. Concurrently, rivals and suppliers also moved abroad.

In the final stage of the cycle, the enterprise, having lost its competitive advantage, took one of four actions. It either dropped the product, created a new advantage by altering the product, created the image of a new product through advertising, or sought the lowest-cost production site from which to service both foreign and U.S. markets. So production shifted to low-labor-cost countries, e.g., less developed countries. One of the main advantages of this theory is its ability to explain the investment by U.S. firms first in the developed countries and much later the shift to developing economies.

In addition, Vernon's approach helps to explain the choice of foreign investment over exporting to service an overseas market. He argues that if average local production costs equaled marginal costs at home plus transportation costs, a company would commence foreign production. Thus, foreign investment is seen as a function of economies of scale and growth in local markets. He also improves on Hymer's theory in that for Hymer the nationality of a MNC was an historic accident. Vernon explains the nationality of a MNC in terms of national market characteristics which give rise to proprietary advantages for companies close to the market. Finally, Vernon's theory makes a partial explanation of cross investment but only by companies in different industries or in the same industries at different stages of the product life cycles.

Aliber (1970) considers whether direct investment could be better explained as a currency area or a customs area phenomenon. He endeavors to build a theory that would eliminate the deficiencies of earlier explanations, e.g., inability to predict country or industry patterns of investment, inadequate explanations of foreign takeovers, and lack of integration with alternative forms of serving foreign markets such as licensing and exporting. Taking as his starting point a source-country firm with some monopolistic advantage (patent) and a unified currency area, he analyzes the decision to service a foreign market via direct investment, licensing, or export. In this case, he found that the choice of how to service a foreign market depended on the size of foriegn market (economies of scale) and the height of tariffs.

Next, assuming a unified customs area, Aliber considers the effect of multiple currencies on foreign direct-investment patterns. In this case, he finds that the choice between exporting and direct investment depended on the costs of doing business abroad and national differences in capitalization rates, not tariff heights. He suggests two reasons for such differences. First, the market demanded a premium for having uncertainty about exchange risk; and second, the market applied a higher capitalization rate to the same income stream when earned by a source-country firm than a host-country firm. To summarize, Aliber (1970) postulates: (1) the pattern of foreign versus domestic exploitation of a patent is a function of the height of tariffs in a certain area; (2) the pattern of host-source country of investment is a function of differences in the capitalization of identical income streams in different currencies; (3) the pattern of foreign investment versus licensing is a function of capitalization ratios of foreign versus local firms; and (4) the pattern of foreign investment intensive industries is a function of the capital intensity of different industries.

Criticisms of Aliber's approach center on two main issues. First, he assumes that a local firm and a MNC earn the same income from a given "patent". This implicitly assumes perfect information in the patent market and that monopoly profits are undiluted when a patent is sold. At the least, this ignores advantages due to national endowments or to the structure of a MNC. Second, Aliber assumes differential capitalization rates are a function of the currency premium. As such, they result from the macroeconomic environment of the company. It has been suggested that the rates would be better formulated as a function of the industry and company characteristics of the MNC.

The last major theory, that of Servan-Schreiber, is a limited subset of Hymer's approach with the competitive advantage based on the superior creativity of U.S. management. This theory assumes that management skills are culture bound and that the MNC can use this to advantage if it can apply previously successful management techniques to local conditions. Evidence that conglomerates are not typically MNCs implies a management advantage must be combined with another advantage to explain foreign investment.

Having presented the major theories of foreign direct investment, a review of their empirical validity follows.

Empirical Tests of Positive Theories

Numerous studies have been conducted to test the explanatory power of various positive theories of foreign direct investment. One by Caves (1974) tested three explanations which he calls: (1) intangible assets, (2) multiplant enterprise, and (3) entrepreneurial resources. These are all variants of Hymer's thesis that foreign direct investment results from monopolistic advantages due to market imperfections. These advantages accrue from product differentiation in the intangible asset case, economies of scale in the multiplant enterprise case, and management expertise in the entrepreneurial resources case. The last case is the Servan-Schreiber approach.

Caves tested these approaches by seeing how well they explained the variation of share of sales in various Canadian and U.K. manufacturing industries accounted for by foreign-owned firms. He used multiple-regression analysis on a sample of 67 Canadian industries over the period 1965-1967 and 36 U.K. industries.

Caves found slightly differing results for the Canadian and U.K. samples. For Canada, of the intangible asset variables, he found that research and development as a percentage of sales was always significant. Advertising as a percentage of sales was significant as well, lending support to the product differentiation approach. A variant of the intangible asset theory was the importance that firm size and barriers to entry had for explaining direct investment. The proxy for this approach was always significant as was the proxy for the multiplant operations theory. He found no support for the entrepreneurial resources approach. In the U.K. sample, Caves found that R&D and advertising remained significant, but the multiplant variable was far less significant than in Canadian investment.

As a further test for each sample, Caves subdivided the industries into consumer and producer goods. Rerunning the regressions, he found that investment in consumer goods was best explained by product differentiation (intangible asset) variables, while producer-good investment was more responsive to entry barriers and location (multiplant) variables.

Several earlier studies of foreign direct investment had focused not on the variables explaining the commitment of resources abroad, but rather on the characteristics of industries or firms involved in foreign operations. In an extensive survey of the industry-oriented literature, Caves concluded:

> In the parlance of industrial organization, oligopoly with product differentiation normally prevails where corporations make "horizontal" investments abroad. Oligopoly, not necessarily differentiated in the home market, is typical in industries which undertake "vertical" direct investments. (1971, p. 1)

Based on a study of 187 multinational firms, Vernon (1971) reached similar conclusions. He found that multinationals tend to be larger, more profitable, more advertising- and research-oriented, and more diversified than firms less heavily involved abroad.

In an attempt to synthesize the firm and industry approaches, Horst (1972) focused on factors which might differentiate investors from noninvestors in a given industry. He considered factors such as firm size, degree of vertical integration, profitability, capital to labor ratio, advertising intensity, R&D effort, and product diversity as discriminating characteristics of companies investing abroad. Using regression analysis on a sample of 1,191 manufacturing companies and the 187 MNCs by the Harvard Business School designation (see Vernon, 1971) for 1967, he concluded that once industry factors were excluded, the only differentiating factor between investors and noninvestors was firm size.

As a second step, holding firm-size constant, Horst examined industry factors of foreign direct investors. He found that the level of R&D expenditures was significant, lending support to the subset of Hymer's market imperfections theory, the intangible asset approach tested by Caves. Additionally, he found support for the economies of scale or multiplant enterprise explanation tested by Caves.

Scaperlanda and Mauer (1969) also tested the economies of scale hypothesis which they called the market size hypothesis, as well as a growth and tariff discrimination explanation of direct investment in the European Economic Community (E.E.C.) (The tariff discrimination approach is an example of Hymer's market imperfections caused by government interference.) Applying regression analysis to data on U.S. direct investment for 1952-1966, they found that the only significant variable in every case was market size, the proxy for the economies of scale theory.

In subsequent work, Goldberg (1972) disputed the Scaperlanda and Mauer results, finding that market growth, not size, was the prime explanatory variable of U.S. investment in the E.E.C. Goldberg used data spanning the same period as the earlier research, but he recast the tariff discrimination and growth variables. The tariff variable remained insignificant.

As noted by Ray (1977), these early studies of foreign direct investment gave conflicting results partly because they did not contain explicit derivations of foreign direct investment equations. He set out to do this by developing a model based on profit-maximizing behavior and incorporating a constant returns to scale, homogeneous, transcendental logarithmic production function. The derivation of the investment model indicated that in perfect competition, optimal investment would be independent of domestic production and exports. Ray tested this empirically and found that exports were a significant variable in the model. Thus, he concluded some degree of imperfection existed between foreign and domestic markets and that his model was consistent with the defensive theories of direct investment, i.e., Vernon's product life-cycle approach.

In another attempt to model the foreign investment process at the aggregate level, Boatwright and Renton (1975) utilized the neoclassical theory of optimal capital accumulation. The approach required two steps. First was to specify the desired level of capital stock, assuming that firms seek to maximize profits. The second step was to specify the adjustment of the actual stock to the desired stock. Investment was viewed as two types—replacement, which was assumed proportional to the current capital stock, and net investment, which depended on the relative capital costs and production functions at home and abroad. Since it takes time to adjust to changes in desired capital stock, alternative lagged-adjustment models were specified for empirical testing. The data for fitting the models ran quarterly from 1961 to 1972 and consisted of U.K. foreign direct-investment inflows and outflow.

They found in estimating the lagged adjustment of actual to desired capital stock that Alman and Pascal distributions were unsatisfactory. The best model approximations were made by a geometric lag adjustment, coupled with a greater than unity elasticity of substitution between labor and capital and increasing return to scale in the production function. They concluded that the neoclassical model provided a reasonable explanation of direct investment in the aggregate, but that it had not been tested against alternative theories.

One attempt to do such comparative testing, but which does not include the neoclassical theory, is a work by Wesche (1974). He tests the explanatory power of the six theories detailed at the outset of this section for a sample of German direct, private investments (DPI) by 34 industries. Using multiple-regression techniques, he found that:

1. The differential interest rate theory remains without empirical support. This is consistent with its restricted theoretical explanatory potential.
2. The growth-of-the-firm theory appears to make a marginal contribution to a full explanation of DPI. Exceptional growth rates can raise an industry's DPI level, but not modify its propensity.
3. The theories of Hymer, Vernon, Aliber, and Servan-Schreiber test out as significant DPI explanations. This is quite consistent with their theoretical potential. They alone envision an imperfect market structure for DPI transfers, where various proprietary abilities of DPI firms are unattainable to indigenous competitors, and where their monopolistic returns are high enough to overcome the inherent cost advantages of local competitors. (Wesche, 1974, pp. 162-64)

Thus, although considerable testing of alternative theories of foreign direct investment has been conducted, no clearcut superiority of one approach has emerged. As Caves (1974) critiques,

> much of the copious literature on the multinational firm, whether positive or normative, approaches its subject with neither an analytical model of how the beast operates nor a systematic test of the model's predictions. (p. 280)

The present research attempts to make a beginning of this within the context of a positive analysis of firm decision-making. The approach is micro in orientation; i.e., it looks at specific firms, not aggregate data. To place the present research in the proper context, the following chapter reviews the literature on foreign direct investment at the firm level.

3
Investment Decisions of the MNC: Firm Approach

Investigations of foreign direct-investment behavior with a single-firm focus fall into two categories: normative and positive studies. Normative research is by far the larger group and tends to be found in textbooks on international financial management. Positive approaches are usually questionnaire surveys of the reasons why companies make direct investments. Since the normative group is by far the larger of the two, the following chapter begins with a review of the predominant opinions on how firms ought to make foreign investment decisions.

Normative Theories of Firm International Investment Decisions

The investment decision of a multinational firm is more complicated than that of a domestic company, due to the added complexity of the international environment. The interaction of such factors as exchange rate fluctuations, differential tax structures, differential inflation rates, and multiple legal and political systems makes the application of traditional domestic investment decision methods difficult. As Piper (1971) puts it:

> *The relative stability of the U.S. political, social, economic, and legal milieu reduces such factors to constants for all practical purposes. The decision maker thus begins with a smaller and less complex series of variables which he must subject to analysis.* Moreover, since the social-legal-political environment is relatively constant, he is able to focus upon what are largely commercial variables. These often are relatively easy to quantify and to investigate from abundant and available statistical data. In short, the domestic investor, confronted with a relatively small number of decision variables and the prospect of being able to analyze those variables in a rational way, has a reasonably good chance of becoming an intelligent risk taker, that is, of identifying and measuring an investment risk.
>
> The same chances of success, however, are most often greatly reduced when the manager considers expansion into foreign markets, particularly in the developing areas. *Two factors complicate his risk analysis in this case: (1) the social, political, and legal variables dormant in the U.S. investment decision are activated.* These are often difficult to identify and to deal with in quantitative form; and *(2) the commercial variables become more difficult to quantify in the absence of sophisticated economic and commercial data.* (pp. 1-2)

In addition to the greater complexity of the decision environment, the existence of parent-subsidiary relationships further exacerbates the problem of using domestic capital-budgeting techniques in the international investment decision. For example, whose cash flows, parent or subsidiary, are relevant for decision-making? Whose cost of capital should be employed if a discounted cash flow technique is employed? How should system-wide costs or benefits be analyzed? What are the appropriate acceptance criteria for foreign investment? Normative theories of direct investment seek to answer these questions and to recommend methods for handling the unique risks of foreign investments (i.e., foreign currency and political risk).

One of the earliest normative approaches to direct investment was a 1968 article by Stonehill and Nathanson (1968). On theoretical and empirical grounds they rejected long-run profit maximization of profits as the goal of foreign investment decision-making. They argued for a behavioral theory of decision-making, and in this context the appropriate acceptance criterion for an international investment should be that it generates a positive net present value from the parent perspective, the subsidiary perspective, and for the home and host countries (on a social cost/benefit basis). To this end, they concluded that: (1) the parent company should discount cash flows by *its weighted average cost of capital under its optimal capital structure,* as should the subsidiary, and since the optimal capital structures may differ for each, so may the cost of capital; (2) incremental cash inflow from the parent perspective should include dividends, royalties, interest and loan repayments, export profits, and terminal value of the subsidiary, while cash outflows should equal all equity and loan capital to the subsidiary; (3) incremental cash inflow for the subsidiary should include earnings after tax but before depreciation, royalties, or interest payments, while outflows should equal the original investment in assets; and (4) an allowance for political and foreign currency risk should be made by charging cash flows for the cost of uncertainty absorption whether or not undertaken. They argued against the commonly advocated practice of using a higher cost of capital for foreign investments because this method does not allow for the actual amount of risk nor the time pattern of uncertainty.

Several alternative ways to account for international risks have been advocated by other authors. For example, Dymsza (1972) proposed either (1) compiling subjective risk indices for each country of planned investment and then adjusting the required cutoff rate to reflect this risk or (2) constructing a composite risk factor reflecting the country investment climate and project risks based on uncertainty of cash flows and then using this factor to discount projected cash flows. But Zenoff and Zwick (1969) argued that adjusting the discount rate to reflect risk for an international investment is an inadequate and arbitrary approach, in part because it implicitly assumes that risks are the same before and after investment.

They favored hypothesizing alternative scenarios, including the impact of possible exchange rates and political developments on receipts, disbursements, and required inflows and outflows, and then assigning probabilities to each scenario. Using a constant cost of capital[1] they calculated an expected net present value for each project. They combined this expected return with a subjective risk estimate to be evaluated with the use of utility curves in selecting which investments should be made.

This probability analysis approach to incorporate foreign currency and political risks into investment analysis is advocated by a number of authors [see Zwick (1967), Gaddis (1966), and Stobaugh (1969)], including Rodriquez and Carter (1976). However, they took the analysis one step further. Using the dispersion of returns as a measure of risk, they advocated using a risk-return preference aproach to the final decision outcome.

Returning to the issue of whose cash flow and cost of capital are relevant to investment evaluation, not all authors agree with Stonehill and Nathanson that both parent and subsidiary perspectives are important. For example, Dymsza (1972) stressed that the best method for evaluating overseas investments is net present value from a parent perspective. Thus, the appropriate concept of income would be net profits (adjusted for losses of licensing or export income displaced by local production, management fees, interest on loans, etc., and any synergistic effects) after tax to the parent. Zenoff and Zwick (1969) agreed with this parent perspective. So does Bugnion (1972).

There is much disagreement on the appropriate acceptance criteria for foreign investments. As mentioned earlier, Stonehill and Nathanson (1968) advocated using a net present value criterion while Zenoff and Zwick (1969) and Rodriquez and Carter (1976) proposed using utility functions. Bugnion utilized an internal rate of return approach.

Bugnion (1972) attempted to develop an international capital-budgeting model which adapted the internal rate of return (IRR) concept to two fundamental characteristics of the multinational corporation; namely, its financial duality and its multiplicity of political and economic environments. He recognized the first by stressing that investment evaluation be done at parent headquarters so that a company can incorporate into the analysis of cash flows to the parent the effects of transfer pricing, the impact of other subsidiary investment decisions, and the consideration of global tax effects.

The second characteristic was recognized by adjusting cash flows for the effects of likely changes in the overseas environment—e.g., inflation, devaluation, and nationalization by use of probability analysis on each element of cash flow. An IRR was then calculated for each project.

Bugnion then estimated the cost of capital for each subsidiary wishing to undertake a project. The final step in his procedure was to calculate a net rate of return, the difference between a project's IRR and cost of capital. He advocated accepting projects in order of decreasing net return on investment until available financings were exhausted.

To summarize, normative theories of foreign direct investment seek to guide firms in analyzing the unique aspects of international investments, i.e., political and foreign currency risks and parent-subsidiary relationships. In general, they attempt to apply domestic capital-budgeting techniques to the more complex international sphere, and as the preceding review indicates there are several unresolved areas. However, in his synthesis of the normative literature, Bavishi (1979) produced the following set of theoretically prescribed methods for analyzing foreign direct investments:

1. *Cash flows* should be evaluated from either the parent's or the subsidiary's perspective as long as the underlying assumptions are satisfied.
2. *Discounted cash flow methods* (i.e., internal rate of return or net present value) should be used for analyzing project cash flows.
3. *Indirect benefits* of overseas investments should be measured along with cash flows, since these benefits eventually will have tangible effects on either the projects or the company's cash flows.
4. MNCs should use their worldwide weighted average *cost of capital* for evaluating investment projects.
5. The *range of risk variables considered* should be broadened and evaluated using management science techniques . . . probability analysis, sensitivity analysis, simulation models, and decision free analysis.
6. The *allowance for risk* . . . should be done . . . [either by computing] certainty equivalent cash flows . . . [or by using] risk adjusted discount rates to reflect the relative uncertainty of various cash streams of the project. (pp. 6-8)

Although a number of methods for analyzing the complexities of international environments have been proposed, the positive research will make clear that none has gained general acceptance. Before turning to the positive studies, the importance of political and currency risks in international operations requires that developments in these fields be given a brief review.

Political Risk

One of the better treatments of political risk as it applies to business operations overseas is found in a 1971 article by S.H. Robock (1971). Robock made an important distinction between political risk and political instability. According to him, political risk exists when discontinuities occur in the business environment, when they are difficult to anticipate, and when they result from a political change. To constitute a risk, these changes in the environment must have a potential for significantly affecting the profit or other goals of an enterprise.

From this definition, Robock presented the schemata of the sources and effects of political risk (1971) (see Table 2). One of Robock's main contributions was his emphasis on forecasting political risk and quantifying its impact on a company's operations. His approach included four steps: (1) understanding the government's power source, behavior, and stability; (2) analyzing the company's products for vulnerability to change in the business environment generated from political changes; (3) determining the source of political risk; and (4) projecting the time, probability, and effect of political risk on cash flows. He advocated calculating an expected net present value weighted by the probabilities of political changes to quantify political risk.

Robock's article focused directly on political risk as it relates to overseas business. However, the preponderance of research on political risk has been conducted by political scientists and has been aimed at developing indices of political risk for various countries. Some of these indices have been used by companies as measures of political risk. The four most widely recognized indices are the Russet Measure, the Banks and Textor Measure, the Feierabend Index, and the Haner Index.[2]

Green and Korth (1974) compared the first three measures and selected the Feierabend Index as the most useful for business purposes. Their recommendation came from the fact that this index is far more comprehensive and flexible than the other two and because it lends itself to prediction as well as comparative rankings. In addition, the data come in disaggregated form, which allows the decision-maker to exercise judgment on the importance of various factors in specific countries and/or individual projects.

One research effort on foreign investments which employed the Feierabend Index was a study by R.T. Green (1971). He tested five hypotheses regarding the relationship between political instability (as measured by the Feierabend Index) and foreign marketing investment. He hypothesized: (1) a negative relationship between foreign direct investment and political instability; (2) a less negative relationship for large markets than for small; (3) a less negative relationship between investment and political instability for Latin America than for other less developed countries; (4) that the flow of direct investment would be related to short-term political instability rather than long-term effects; and (5) that long-term instability would be a better predictor of future instability than short-term instability. For U.S. foreign investment data from 1958 to 1965, only hypothesis three could be tentatively accepted.

Table 2

Political Risk: A Conceptual Framework

Sources of Political Risk	Groups Through Which Political Risk Can Be Generated	Political Risk Effects: Types of Influence on International Business Operations
Competing political philosophies (nationalism, socialism, communism)	Government in power and its operating agencies	Confiscation: loss of assets without compensation
Social unrest and disorder	Parliamentary opposition groups	Expropriation with compensation: loss of freedom to operate
Vested interests of local business groups	Nonparliamentary opposition groups (Algerian "FLN," guerrilla movements working from within or outside of country)	Operational restrictions: market shares, product characteristics, employment policies, locally shared ownership, etc.
Recent and impending political independence	Nonorganized common interest groups: students, workers, peasants, minorities, etc.	Loss of transfer freedom (e.g., dividends, interest payments), goods, personnel or ownership rights
Armed conflicts and internal rebellions for political power	Foreign governments or intergovernmental agencies such as the EEC	Breaches or unilateral revisions in contracts and agreements
New international alliances	Foreign governments willing to enter into armed conflict or to support internal rebellion	Discrimination such as taxes, compulsory subcontracting
		Damage to property or personnel from riots, insurrections, revolutions, and wars

Only a limited amount of research to date relates political instability directly with foreign investment behavior. Similarly, most of the literature on foreign exchange risk has developed apart from direct-investment research.

Foreign Exchange Risk

Following the announcement of FASB No. 8,[3] a great deal of attention recently has been focused on accounting definitions of exchange risk [see Harrigan (1976), Teck, (1974), and Snyder (1977)]. These definitions are concerned primarily with which assets and liabilities in the foriegn subsidiary's financial statements should be considered exposed to currency fluctuations. The most common approaches advocated for translating overseas accounts are the all-current, current/noncurrent, and monetary/nonmonetary methods. The FASB requires use of the temporal approach which, under present accounting practices, is equivalent to the monetary-nonmonetary approach. This method translates monetary assets (cash and receivables) and monetary liabilities (payables and debt) at current exchange rates. All other accounts are translated at historical rates. From an accounting perspective, a firm's translation exposure is the difference between monetary assets and liabilities.

Recognizing that this concept leaves out important sources of foreign currency risk, several authors have suggested alterations to better reflect a firm's economic exposure. Teck (1974) added in transaction exposure (transactions denominated in other than parent-company currency) to translation exposure. Gull (1975) developed a composite measure of exchange risk. Emphasizing the correlations between currencies, he employed a portfolio approach to exchange-risk management. Heckerman (1972) evaluated exchange risks in foreign operations using a discounted present-value approach.

The problem with all of these approaches is that they failed to examine explicitly the effects that a currency fluctuation has on the future cash flows of the MNC. Shapiro and Rutenberg (1976) laid out the possible demand and cost effects of currency changes in terms of local demand, foreign demand, costs of local inputs, and cost of foreign inputs. They believed that dissecting exchange risk in this manner enables the firm to determine more precisely its possible losses due to currency changes. Shapiro and Rutenberg advocated using probability estimates with these disaggregated cash flows in a chance-constrained hedging decision approach. In this context, the goal of exchange-risk management is to limit the probability of losing more than a specified amount in any given period.

A variety of other approaches to foreign currency management have been suggested,[4] and a considerable body of research has been devoted to defining, measuring, and managing foreign exchange and political risks. Although most all normative theories of foreign direct investment advocate incorporating these risks into the investment decision, the following review of positive research shows that they generally have not been adequately included.

Positive Theories of Firm International Investment Decisions

In 1971 Piper conducted a survey of the decision methods of 22 U.S. multinationals which applied for AID investment assistance. The survey uncovered 38 decision variables which fell into five categories: financial considerations, technical/engineering feasibility considerations, marketing considerations, economic/legal considerations, and political/social considerations. Piper found that financial and technical/engineering considerations were given by far the greatest emphasis. Political/social considerations were hardly ever mentioned as important, and little comparative analysis was undertaken. He attributed the emphasis on technical/engineering factors to study team bias. (The consistency of these findings with a behavioral theory approach will be discussed in the next chapter.)

In another survey study, Kim (1976) examined the financial motives for direct investment in Korea. His sample included 41 of the 96 U.S. companies with operations in Korea as of December 1973. He found that the motivation for investment was more often low wages than a high-enough rate of return. The main evaluation method was a payback, not a discounted cash flow approach as advocated by normative theorists. For companies using a discounted cash flow evaluation criterion, devaluation risk was accounted for by using a minimum required rate of return, not by requiring returns greater than domestic returns.

Richardson developed an objective function in terms of potential profit from producing in a given market and a spatial preference measure. He produced investment decision curves which depended on target returns, price, and spatial preference. It was within the spatial preference parameter that exchange rate and political risks were captured. He utilized the decision-curve framework to explain the movement from export to overseas production.

In his concluding remarks, Richardson commented on the difficulty of testing a framework like his which incorporates both economic and subjective variables. He states that "what is required is detailed studies of individual firm's foreign investment history" (Richardson, 1971, p. 19).

Such a comprehensive history is provided by the research of Aharoni (1966). However, because his research is closely intertwined with the behavioral theory approach to firm decision, it will be reviewed in the next chapter.

4

Traditional Versus Behavioral Theory of Firm Decisions

Introducing their behavior theory approach to firm decision making, Cyert and March (1962) made the following justifications for a departure from classical economic theory.

> Assuming that the firm is operating within a perfectly competitive market, the generally received theory asserts that the objective of the firm is to maximize net revenue in the face of given prices and a technologically determined production function. . . . Existing theory of the firm treats two main areas—the conditions for maximum net revenue, and the analysis of shifts in equilibrium positions . . . the theory has been extended to cover either imperfect factor markets, imperfect product markets or both (e.g., the theory of monopolistic competition and oligopoly theory). These elaborations, while extending the theory to new market situations retain the basic framework and decision making process postulated for the firm in perfect competition.
>
> Dissatisfaction with this limited revision has led to a reexamination of the basic theory of the firm itself. . . . Two major difficulties [are] perceived by economists who view the basic theory as deficient. First, the motivational and cognitive assumption of the theory appear unrealistic. Profit maximization . . . is either only one among many goals of business firms or not a goal at all. . . . The classical assumption of certainty and its modern equivalent—knowledge of the probability distribution of future events—have been challenged. Second, the "firm" of the theory has few of the characteristics we have come to identify with actual business firms. (pp. 5-8)

A substantial body of literature has addressed the limitations in the assumptions of the traditional theory of firm behavior. First, the research of Scitovsky (1943), Reder (1947), Fellner (1949), Williamson (1963), Baumol (1959), Boulding (1950), and others explored alternatives to profit maximization as the goal of business activity. They found that such variables as leisure, control, security, growth, market share, sales, and asset ratios were viable from goals. Second, work by Simon (1952), Homans (1950), and Barnard (1956) examined firm decision-making under uncertainty, rejecting the classical assumptions of certainty or probability distributions in favor of the concept Simon termed "bounded rationality." Finally, a large body of research developed by Weber (1947), Merton (1957), Barnard (1956), Simon (1952), Margolis (1959), and others rejected the entrepreneurial firm as a description of the modern firm in favor of an organizational focus.

Consistent with this research, Cyert and March (1962) sought to remedy deficiencies in the traditional theory of the firm by constructing a theory that took

> (1) the firm as its basic unit, (2) the prediction of firm behavior with respect to decisions such as price, output and resource allocation as its objective, and (3) an explicit emphasis on the actual process of organizational decision making as its basic research commitment. (1962, p. 19)

Their resultant analytical framework consisted of three main variables and four major relational concepts. They proposed that modern business decison-making could be analyzed in terms of the factors impacting organizational goals, organizational expectations, and organizational choice. Their relational concepts included quasiresolution of conflict, uncertainty avoidance, problematic search, and organizational learning.

As opposed to the traditional theory of an entrepreneurial firm, Cyert and March viewed the firm as a coalition of groups with disparate desires and preferences. They identified two sets of variables impacting firm goals. The first set influenced what was considered important by the firm.[1] Included in this set were such factors as the members in the coalition, the locus of decision-making, and the definition of the problem facing the firm. The second set of factors influenced the aspiration level on any goal and included the group's past goals, past performance, and the past performance of comparable groups. As envisaged by Cyert and March, the goals of the firm include sales, inventory, production, market share, and profit goals.

Cyert and March viewed organizational expectation as resulting from drawing inferences from available information. Thus, the key variables impacting firm expectations were those affecting the process of drawing inferences, the ways in which information became available to the firm, and how information was communicated within the firm. These were primarily factors affecting the intensity, success, and direction of the search activity of the firm, e.g., the nature of the problem stimulating search, the location in the firm where search is focused.

This organizational approach to expectation formulation differs from the pure theory of expectations. The traditional approach views investment and resource allocation decisiions as maximization problems equating marginal revenues and costs. As such, organizations are viewed as scanning all alternatives and continuously adjusting investment portfolios based on accurate information on costs and returns. In this manner, an optimal allocation of resources is achieved. Modern theory replaces certain information with probability distributions of expected returns.

Cyert and March raised several objections to this formulation. First, empirical research has indicated that firm decision-making is better characterized by what Stobaugh calls "go-no go" analysis rather than comparisons of multiple alternatives. Second, the traditional theory of expectations views search just as an alternative use of resources. Research by Simon (1959) and others has cast doubt on this formulation of search activity. Third, the computational requirements of the traditional theory are so large as to be nearly impossible for most firms, even with the use of computers. Most important, expectations are given that are not explained by the theory. Cyert and March explicitly address formulation of expectations within the firm as a key element of their analytical framework.

As a major element of their framework, Cyert and March identified three variables impacting organizational choice. The first was how the problem facing the firm was defined. The second was what standard decision rules were used to solve the problem. The third was in what order the alternatives were presented, which was found to depend on the part of the organization that was making the decision, and past experience in considering alternatives. They derived three fundamental rules characterizing firm choice: (1) avoid uncertainty; (2) maintain rules; and (3) use simple rules.

In addition to these major variables impacting firm decision-making, Cyert and March detailed four relational concepts. The first concept was that of quasiresolution of conflict. Contrary to traditional approaches, they argued that the process of resolving conflict among the members of the coalition (firm) did not result in internally consistent goals. They postulated that this process used three means to resolve conflict: (1) *local rationality*—the firm divided problems and assigned them to specific groups so that any single unit dealt with a limited number of problems and goals; (2) *acceptable level decision rules*—the firm underexploited the environment, resulting in excess resources to absorb inconsistency; and (3) *sequential attention to goals*—resulting in a time buffer for dealing with inconsistencies.

The second relational concept was that of uncertainty avoidance. Cyert and March found that rather than anticipate future events, firms sought to avoid uncertainty (and so the need to predict) through the use of plans, standard operating procedures, industry tradition, and by arranging a negotiated environment.

The third relational concept was that of problematic search. With respect to organizational search, Cyert and March assumed that:

1. Search was motivated by a problem and would end once a solution was found.

2. Search was simpleminded, being based on the two rules of searching for solutions first in the area of the problem and in the area of the current alternative.
3. Search was biased by the training, experience, hopes, expectations, and uresolved conflicts of the subgroup making the investigation.

The final relational concept is that of organizational learning. Cyert and March contended that firms exhibited adaptation in terms of goals, attention rules, and search rules. Regarding goals, they assumed that firm objectives were a function of past goals as well as the firm's and similar groups' past experience with goals. As such, goals change over time. Also, they asserted that firms learn to focus attention on certain aspects and measures of their environment and to ignore others. Finally, Cyert and March expected that firms would learn which search rules worked and which did not, and so these rules would change over time.

The basic framework—the three variables of goals, choice, and expectation, and the four relational concepts—has been tested in numerous studies.[2] As Cyert and March noted, "the natural theoretical language for describing a process involving such phenomena is the language of a computer program" (1962, p. 125). Applying their framework via computer simulation, they modeled the price and output decisions of a retail department store. They described two goals for the department, a sales and markup goal, and specified learning behavior in goals and aspiration levels from feedback. They empirically tested the model's price and output estimates and found that the model predicted well.

The most comprehensive support from the international field for the behavioral theory came from Aharoni's (1966) case studies of 38 companies that had considered direct investment in Israel. He studied the organizational factors that influenced foreign investment decisions and the impact of information availability, communication, and use in the decision process. His goal was to explain and predict behavior in order to gauge firm reaction to stimulus to investment; i.e., his research had a policy formulation focus.

Aharoni found that the major initiating forces for foreign investment were strong interest of an executive, an outside proposal, a threat to a lucrative market, the "bandwagon effect" (1966, pp. 65-68), and the desire to countermove against foreign competitors' invasion of the domestic market. In his inquiries into the investigation process, Aharoni found that companies made decisions in terms of a specific project in a specific country and that they did not compare several countries seeking the best alternative. This result supported Cyert and March's relational concept of problematic search. The importance of organizational expectations in the foreign decision process was highlighted by Aharoni in his analysis of the impact of the initiating force on the decision outcome. He found that the variables to be investigated and the scope of the investigation depended largely on the magnitude of the initiating force as well as the perception of the problem by the investigator. Uncertainty avoidance was found to be a prominent factor in the decision process. Aharoni noted that initial screening of investments centered around crude estimates of risk.

Although most of Aharoni's results fit well into the behavioral theory approach of Cyert and March, two findings did not. First, Aharoni found that leadership was an important force in the decision process. The Cyert and March framework with its emphasis on coalitions and organizational slack precluded a role for leadership in business decisions. Also, Aharoni found that the search for information created commitments which could bias information and in itself compel the firm to decide in a certain way. The behavioral theory as outlined by Cyert and March largely ignored commitment.

Based on his research, Aharoni constructed a variant of the behavioral framework for firm decisions. He retained the relational concepts of Cyert and March: quasiresolution of conflict, uncertainty avoidance, problematic search, and organizational learning. However, he formulated alternatives to the variables of goals, expectations, and choice. He postulated that the investment decision should be analyzed in terms of (1) structure, (2) participants, (3) interactions, and (4) information (Aharoni, 1966, pp. 292-300).

Important variables in the structure category included diverse individual goals, coalitions, and leadership leading to organizational goals, participant roles oriented toward fulfilling goals, and organizational stability. Key aspects in the participant category included individual attitudes, values, roles, and commitments which constrained future action. The main factor in the interactions group was the continuous process of mutual bargaining and influence. Finally, key variables in the information category included costs in terms of management time, uncertainty, and commitments.

In summary, Aharoni concluded

> a foreign investment decision is a very complicated social process. . . . It contains various elements of individual and organizational behavior, influenced by the past and the perception of the future as well as by the present. It is composed of a large number of decisions, made by different people at different points in time. The understanding of the final outcome of such a process depends on an understanding of all its stages and parts. (1966, pp. 45-46)

With this in mind, the present study seeks to expand the understanding of the international investment decision process by focusing on actual behavior. The next chapter describes the methodology of the study.

5
Methodology

Overview

The research described here is a positive inquiry into the international investment behavior and decision processes of multinational corporations. That is, it seeks to describe how such firms actually make foreign investment decisions. The specific goals of the research are to:

1. Document the international investment motives and evaluation practices used by a sample of U.S.-based manufacturing MNCs.
2. Discover the significant variables and relationships between variables in the international investment decision process of MNCs.
3. Test hypotheses on international investment decision-making drawn from the traditional and the behavioral theory frameworks.

The methodology chosen to accomplish these objectives is a questionnaire survey of a sample of MNCs in conjunction with a field study of selected questionnaire respondents.

The need for additional positive research on the decision to invest abroad has been demonstrated in the literature review in earlier chapters of this book. For example, as Aharoni concluded,

> There is certainly a pressing need for a meaningful theory that will help management improve its practices. A prerequisite for such a theory, however, is that it will indeed be a usable vehicle for improvements. To be usable, a normative theory should not prescribe unattainable goals, based on unrealistic conditions. Instead, the environment in which business operates the society around it, and the personalities, roles, values and goals of the participants in the system must all be incorporated in the analysis to make the conclusions and prescriptions meaningful and operative. (1966, p. 28)

In order to obtain the breadth and richness of information necessary, a questionnaire survey and follow-up are appropriate research methods.

The questionnaire was designed to survey the motives and investment evaluation methods of a sample of U.S.-based manufacturing firms. The sample consisted of all *Fortune 500* companies in 1977 that controlled subsidiaries in six or more countries, a total of 255 companies. Responses to the questionnaire were used to document current practices, screen key variables in the investment decision process, and test hypotheses from the behavioral theory.

Based upon responses to the initial questionnaire, firms to be contacted for the field study were selected. Selection was based on differences in evaluation methods employed, sophistication, industry, size, and country of operation. The purpose of the field work was to explore certain survey responses in depth in order to discover relationships between variables in the international investment decision process. Special attention was given to the organizational context of the decision as prescribed by the behavioral theory framework.

Aharoni's success in using the behavioral approach to analyze foreign investment decisions provided one justification for extending his research. In addition, earlier surveys of MNCs cast doubt on the traditional profit-maximization goal as an objective for direct investment. Desire for growth and market share as well as oligopoly considerations, among other factors, have been uncovered as prime motivators. The geographical spread and organizational complexity of the MNC remove it from the entrepreneurial firm basic to classical theory. Findings by Hymer (1960), Vernon (1972, 1973, 1974), and Horst (1972, 1976) make the assumptions of a competitive market structure for MNC operations seem unrealistic. And the traditional outlook of risk as characterized by probability estimates does not seem to fit well with the complexity of the environments for foreign investment decisions. Nathanson and Stonehill's findings on the use of crude, subjective risk measures by MNCs support this view.

The remainder of the chapter describes in detail the methodology of this research. First is a description of the sample. Next is a general discussion of survey and field study research followed by a detailed description of this study's questionnaire and field study. The next section includes an outline of the anticipated results to be analyzed by the methods described in the last section of this chapter.

Sample Selection

This research is an investigation of the international investment decisions of U.S.-based multinational companies. Accordingly, firms included in the survey sample had to (1) have made an international investment and (2) meet some definition of "multinational company." For operational reasons discussed in the next part of this chapter, the sample was further limited to companies having made a particular type of international investment decision—a foreign direct-investment decision. In contrast to portfolio investment, foreign direct investment implies control of the foreign affiliate by the investor. A 25 percent investment in the voting stock of an affiliate is generally agreed to be sufficient to allow control (Aharoni, 1971). Any U.S. company having acquired a 25 percent share of a foreign affiliate was considered to have met the first requirement for inclusion in the sample under study.

The second requirement for inclusion in the study was that a company be "multinational." As discussed earlier, the term "multinational" is an elusive concept. However, there are two generally agreed-upon characteristics of a multinational company—large size and geographic spread. To operationalize the concepts, the Harvard Multinational Enterprise Project (Vernon, 1971) defined large size as a *Fortune 500* company and geographic spread as operations in at least six foreign countries. This definition has become the most commonly used in research on MNCs [see Vernon (1971), Robbins and Stobaugh (1973b), and Dubin (1976)]. In order to facilitate comparison between the results of this study and those of other research, that same definition of a multinational company was employed.

One further limitation was imposed. Again, for operational reasons discussed in the next section, the research was focused on the foreign direct-investment decisions of U.S.-based multinational companies engaged in *manufacturing*. Thus, to be included in the survey sample a company had to (1) be U.S. based, (2) be engaged in manufacturing as its primary activity, (3) have acquired at least a 25 percent share of a foreign affiliate at some time, (4) be a *Fortune 500* company for the year 1977, and (5) have control of a subsidiary in at least six countries as of 1977. Based on these criteria the survey was sent to 255 companies.

The accuracy of the sample was checked in several ways. First, the 1977 list of *Fortune 500* companies was cross-checked in the *Directory of American Firms Operating in Foreign Countries.* This reference includes only those companies with foreign operations in which American firms have a direct capital investment. It also lists the countries in which each U.S. firm has operations. If a company did not have operations in six or more countries, it was deleted from the sample. Next, corporate annual reports, 10K filings, Moody's *Industrial Manual* (1977), and Standard and Poor's *Corporation Records* (1977) were consulted to determine if the companies actually operated in at least six countries in 1977 and if their ownership was 25 percent or more of the affiliate in each country. Prior to mailing the questionnaire, it was not possible to determine whether or not each of the 255 firms owned *manufacturing* affiliates. However, the questionnaire clearly stated that if a company does not own a 25 percent share of a manufacturing affiliate in six or more countries the questionnaire was to be returned uncompleted. Fifty-three companies did not meet these criteria, leaving a final sample of 202 companies.

Using similar criteria as this study for the 1964-65 *Fortune 500*, the original Harvard research sample encompassed 187 companies (Curhan, Davidson, and Luri, 1977). The companies included in the present research include 149 of the 187 companies in the original Harvard sample. Thirty-eight companies no longer meet the criteria. One hundred and six additional companies now meet the criteria and have been added to the present sample.

The companies included in this study do not incorporate all U.S.-based foreign direct investors. According to the latest census by the Bureau of Economic Analysis (U.S. Department of Commerce, 1966), there are some 3,400 U.S.-based direct investors with 23,000 foreign affiliates. Thus, the results of this study will not be generalizable to all U.S. foreign direct investors.

As of 1975 the U.S. Commerce Department listed a universe of 282 U.S. parent companies that maintained majority ownership of at least one foreign manufacturing affiliate (MOFMA). These parent companies controlled 5,900 majority-owned manufacturing affiliates overseas. The list of these companies is not available for direct comparison with the companies included in this research. However, results for 1975 for the companies included in the Harvard sample compare well with the Commerce Department estimates in terms of the number of affiliates. Harvard's sample included 4,600 MOFMAs versus 5,900 for the Commerce Department sample. The Harvard estimate of sales by MOFMA was 71 percent of the Commerce Department estimate (Curhan, 1977). Given the expanded number of companies included in the present survey, the results here should apply to U.S. parents of MOFMA as well as multinational companies in general.

Inspection of the list of companies included in the sample (see Appendix A) indicates that the selection criteria captured the companies generally thought of as multinational. These companies control a large percentage of all U.S. subsidiaries overseas, operate in most foreign countries, and dominate foreign direct investment (Curhan, 1977). As such, they can be considered a representative group of U.S. multinationals.

Survey and Field Study Research

In his book on behavioral research, Kerlinger (1973) delineates two basic types of research, experimental and ex post facto research. Ex post facto research is defined as a

> systematic inquiry in which the scientist does not have direct control of independent variables because their manifestations have already occurred or because they are inherently

not manipulable. Inferences about relations among variables are made, without direct intervention, from concomitant variation of independent and dependent variables. (p. 379)

He further delineates research into laboratory and field research to obtain four broad categories of research: laboratory experiments, field experiments, field studies, and survey research (p. 395). The research of this inquiry is ex post facto in nature and employs both a survey and a field of study.

As Kerlinger puts it, "survey research studies populations by selecting and studying samples chosen from the populations to discover the relative incidence, distribution and interrelations among variables" (p. 410). Survey research seeks factual information including what respondents know about the subject under investigation, what respondents did in the past, and what they are doing now. These purposes of survey research correspond to the goals of the present research, i.e., to document international investment motives and evaluation methods of multinational companies and to discover significant variables and relationships between variables in the decision process.

Kerlinger lists several types of survey approaches: personal interview, telephone interview, panel, and mail questionnaire (p. 414). Of the survey techniques the mail questionnaire has the ability to reach the largest sample at the lowest cost. For these reasons it was selected as the type of survey methodology used in this research. This methodology has been employed by many researchers when the objective of the inquiry was to gain factual information from a large sample of corporations, e.g., the U.S. Department of Commerce (1973), Cutler and Pizer (1964), Klammer (1972), Business International (1974), Kim (1976), Stonehill and Nathanson (1968), Schall et al. (1978), Morsicato (1978), and McInnes (1971).

Kerlinger defines field studies as "ex post facto scientific inquiries aimed at discovering the relations and interactions among variables in real structure" (1973, p. 405). The purpose of a field study is consistent with the objective of the present research, i.e., to discover the relationships between variables in the international investment decision process of MNCs. Katz (1953) further divides field studies into two broad types: exploratory and hypothesis testing. Exploratory studies seek *what is* and have three purposes: to discover significant variables in the field situation, to discover relationships between variables, and to lay the groundwork for later, more rigorous testing of hypotheses. The present research is, thus, primarily exploratory in nature although some limited testing of hypotheses is undertaken.

As Kerlinger notes,

it is well to recognize that there are activities preliminary to hypothesis-testing in research. In order to achieve the desirable aim of hypothesis testing, preliminary methodology and measurement investigation must often be done. The second subtype of exploratory field studies, research aimed at the discovering or uncovering of relations, is indispensable to scientific advance. (1973, p. 406)

It is precisely this type of exploratory study that Carter (1969), Clarkson (1962), and others have stressed is needed in research into corporate financial decision-making and that Aharoni (1966) has indicated is particularly important in international research due to the added complexity of the environment. The present research has as its primary goals the documentation of current practices, the discovery of variables, and the relationships between variables necessary for later hypothesis testing. Thus, exploratory field research is an appropriate methdology. This methodology has been used by other researchers with similar research objectives, e.g., Simon (1947), Cyert and March (1962), Carter (1969), Clarkson (1962), Aharoni (1966), and Cohen (1960).

Both the survey and field study have methodological strengths and weaknesses. The main strength of survey research is its wide scope: a great deal of information can be obtained from a large sample. The amount and quality of information that can be obtained from a survey make it economical.

However, survey research has a significant disadvantage in its inability to probe for depth of information. The present research design takes advantage of the survey's strength—extensive scope—while compensating for its lack of depth by combining the survey with a subsequent field study. As Katz points out,

the field study and survey are not so much alternative ways of studying problems as they are supplementary procedures which can be used most effectively in combination. There are two major advantages in using both methods. First, we know more about the generality from the findings of the field study if we know how the specific situation fits into the [broader] pattern. Secondly, the survey and the field study each produce findings for hypotheses which can be more adequately tested by use of the other approach. (1953, p. 58)

The use of the survey in conjunction with the field study strengthens the overall methodology of this research.

The mail questionnaire as a survey method has strengths and weaknesses itself. The main advantage of a mail questionnaire is its potential for wide distribution at a low cost. Thus, the use of a mail questionnaire reinforces the general advantages of the survey. However, the mail questionnaire has important limitations. The two most prominent are the possible lack of response and the inability to check responses given. Several steps have been taken in the present research to limit the effect of these deficiencies.

In order to improve the response rate, the questionnaire was directed to a targeted individual in each company in the sample. This individual was the chief financial officer or treasurer as identified in either Dun and Bradstreet's *Million Dollar Directory 1977, Standard and Poor's Register of Corporations, Directors and Executives* (1979), or by telephone call to the company. As a second measure to improve the response rate, follow-up questionnaires were mailed to companies that had not answered three weeks after the initial mailing. Next, telephone calls to urge responses were undertaken.

The problem of inability to check responses is diminished somewhat by the field study. Where feasible, factual responses were checked with corporate records and with other persons within the firm. However, in the absence of actual observation of behavior, data about behavior must come from the respondent. Thus, some responses remain unverifiable.

One last limitation of the mail questionnaire is that the instrument must "speak for itself"; i.e., the researcher has no opportunity to amplify or clarify the questions for the respondent and the researcher cannot observe as the respondents answer. Thus, the questionnaire must be designed so that all questions have a clear and common meaning to the respondents and so that the specific questions are getting at the variables intended for research. In order to meet these requirements of questionnaire design, several steps were taken in the present research.

First, the questionnaire was developed out of an extensive literature review. This review enabled the researcher to identify specific problem areas and provided insight to the key variables in the international investment decision process of MNCs. Next, a preliminary questionnaire was presented to several colleagues in various academic disciplines to ascertain the soundness of the basic survey design and the clarity of the wording in each question. Finally, the questionnaire was pretested on the international executives of several MNCs. These companies were former clients of the researcher who voluntarily agreed to participate in the pretest. They represented companies in the major subgroups of the sample. The purpose of the final pretest was to assess potential respondents' evaluation of the project, to verify the clarity and readability of questions, and to isolate possible additions and deletions to the questionnaire.

Attempts were made throughout the research design to diminish the weaknesses of survey research in general and the mail questionnaire in particular. The same holds true for the field study part of the research. According to Kerlinger (1973), ex post facto research has an inherent weakness: lack of control of independent variables. Thus, the major weakness of a field study is that, due to its ex post facto character, statements of relation are weaker than in experimental research. Another methodological weakness is a lower precision in measuring variables due to the greater complexity of field situations.

Katz has suggested two ways to limit the effects of these weaknesses. The first is to delimit clearly the area to be studied and to introduce controls into the data collection process. As he puts it, "It is much more effective to take one central set of variables and investigate them as thoroughly as possible than to try to study the universe in one piece of research" (1953, p. 75). This suggestion has been followed in the present research.

The focus of the investigations has been limited from all international investment decisions of MNCs to initial foreign direct-investment decisions. This eliminates the potentially confounding influence of studying portfolio and reinvestment decisions in the same research as initial foreign direct-investment decisions. Similarly, only manufacturing investment decisions are included in the research. Investment decisions made by service and extractive companies as well as decisions by manufacturing companies or nonmanufacturing opportunities overseas are reserved for future investigations. The study focused on the most recent foreign direct manufacturing investment (FDMI) of a MNC and on the company's practices today in an attempt to control spurious time influences. (A more detailed description of the variables under analysis is contained in the next section of this chapter.)

As a further guard against chance relationships and improper interpretation in field studies, Katz (1953) advises clear and detailed specification of the results the researcher expects to find. Even in exploratory field work, general expectations can be elaborated. The present research has developed several broad hypotheses from the behavioral theory. (A detailed description of the hypotheses follows in a later section of this chapter.) These hypotheses will be tested in the survey and field research and will help achieve the proper interpretation of relationships. But as Katz notes,

> the guarantee applies only to positive or negative findings, not to lack of correlation. If our predictions are borne out fully, then the relationships discovered are not a function of spurious measures or erroneous interpretation but are in all probability a true account of causal connections. (1953, p. 80)

Although the field study has several limitations, it has a number of strengths. Kerlinger (1973) emphasizes that field studies are strong on realism, significance, strength of variables, theory orientation, and heuristic quality. The field study is an observation of real life, and this realism adds strength to the variables and increases external validity. As a study's realism increases, generalizations made from this study to other situations increase. Katz notes that the great advantage of field research is its "inductive procedure, its potentiality for discovering significant variables and basic relations that would never be found if [research] were confined to a hypothetical-deductive model" (1953, p. 75).

Since research into international investment decision-making is a relatively new area, these positive characteristics of field studies are particularly important. The present research design—survey and follow-up field study—has sought to take advantage of these strengths.

The Questionnaire

An extensive literature review in the areas of (1) domestic and international investment decision-making, (2) domestic and international capital budgeting, (3) foreign currency risk, and (4) political risk provided the basis for the development of the questionnaire. This review enabled the researcher to identify areas of controversy, to screen key variables, and to specify precise definitions for the variables under study. As a result, the questionnaire has been divided into four basic sections: (1) foreign investment evaluation practices, (2) international risk analysis methods, (3) company information, and (4) comments. (Appendix B contains the final draft of the questionnaire.)

As a general guide to the respondents in answering questions in each of these four sections, the following definitions were made. First, in order to improve the measurement quality of the variables, the questionnaire sought information only on *foreign direct investments in manufacturing operations*. A foreign direct investment was defined as an equity ownership of at least 25 percent of a foreign operation. If a company's share of a foreign affiliate was less than 25 percent at the time of investment or if the affiliate was not engaged in manufacturing as its primary activity at that time, a respondent was asked not to provide information on that investment.

Second, in order to control as much as possible for time influences in the measurement of variables, the questionnaire sought information on a respondent's *most recent* foreign direct manufacturing investment (FDMI). In the case where more than one FDMI was made in the same year, the respondent was asked to answer for the largest investment made in that year. In that way, the most important FDMI (at least in terms of amount of resources committed) was captured in the survey.

Finally, the questionnaire sought information on the respondents' corporate practices at the time of investment for their most recent FDMI and today. The questionnaire was designed to uncover changes over time (from time of most recent FDMI to today) and to discover if firms employ unique practices for particular investments (e.g., because of the size, activity, or geographic location of the investment). Thus, if a company's practices for evaluating a *typical* potential FDMI today differ from those the company uses today to evaluate a potential investment in the country of its most recent FDMI, then the respondent was asked to answer certain questions with the practices his company would use today to evaluate the typical potential FDMI (typical in terms of size, activity, and geographical area of the potential investment).

The general information requested in Section III of the questionnaire,

Company Information, was intended to provide demographic knowledge about a firm's most recent FDMI. Specifically, information was sought on the geographic area, time period, industry, size, ownership percentage, and method of investment. The information was used in statistical analysis to ascertain the relationships that exist between the demographic variables and the investment evaluation practices and risk analysis methods employed by the MNCs. (The specific statistical analysis used to analyze the survey responses is described in a later section of this chapter.)

Section III also provided knowledge about the structure of the international organization at the time of the firm's most recent FDMI and today, the extensiveness and distribution of the firm's foreign operations, the relationship of the firm's foreign operations to total operations, and the age of a firm as a MNC. These variables were used to determine different degrees of multinational sophistication for the sample and were analyzed for relationships with investment evaluation practices and risk evaluation methods utilized by the firms. Finally, this information was used in testing broad hypotheses drawn from the behavioral theory framework. (Table 3 provides a list of the variables and corresponding questions from Section III of the questionnaire.)

Questions in Section I, Foreign Investment Evaluation Practices, sought first to determine why companies invest in various parts of the world and what general practices they follow in evaluating international investment opportunities. Information was requested on the overall objectives (e.g., profits, growth, etc.) and specific motives (e.g., overcoming tariffs, decreasing labor costs, etc.) for the company's most recent FDMI and a FDMI today. This information was later related to the demographic variables and was needed for testing hypotheses from the behavioral theory.

Second, questions in this section of the questionnaire sought information on the investment evaluation practices companies use. This information was analyzed for relationships with demographic variables and also with objectives and motives for direct investments. The evaluation methods under consideration included for both the most recent FDMI and a FDMI today: who makes direct-investment decisions?, how much comparative analysis does the company undertake?, what financial criteria does the firm use?, how does the corporation measure potential income from a foreign investment opportunity?, how does the company define the cost of capital?, and which currency does the firm use to evaluate foreign direct-investment opportunities? (Table 4 provides a list of the variables and corresponding questions from Section I of the questionnaire.)

The questions in Section II, International Risk Analysis Methods, sought to determine how MNCs analyze the risks in foreign operations. Special attention was given to how they define, analyze, and incorporate into

Table 3

Survey Source of Demographic Information

Variable	Information Source (Section, Question, Part)
I. Demographic	
A. Firm	
1. Age as MNC	Section I, Question 1
2. Industry:	
--today	Compustat tapes
--at time of most recent FDMI	Compustat tapes
3. Organization:	
--today	Section III, Question 3.2
--at time of most recent FDMI	Section III, Question 2
4. Importance of Foreign Operations:	
--today	Section III, Question 3.2
--at time of most recent FDMI	Section III, Question 3.1
5. Distribution of Foreign Operations:	
--today	Section III, Question 4
6. Extensiveness of Foreign Operations:	
--today	Section III, Question 5

Table 3 (Continued)

Variable	Information Source (Section, Question, Part)
B. Most Recent FDMI	
1. Geographic Area	Section III, Question 1A
2. Industry	Section III, Question 1B
3. Method of Investment	Section III, Question 1C.
4. Ownership	Section III, Question 1D
5. Size	Section III, Question 1E
6. Importance	Section III, Question 1E/ Section III, Question 3D and Section III, Question 1E/ Section III, Question 3E

Table 4

Survey Source of Investment Evaluation Practices

Variable	Information Source (Section, Question, Part)
II. Evaluation Practices	
A. Objective of Investment:	
--most recent FDMI	Section I, Question 1
--today	Section I, Question 1.1
	Section I, Question 1.2
B. Motive for Investment:	
--most recent FDMI	Section I, Question 2
--today	Section I, Question 2.1
	Section I, Question 2.2
C. Decision Maker:	
--most recent FDMI	Section I, Question 3
--today	Section I, Question 3.1
	Section I, Question 3.2
D. Comparative Evaluation:	
--most recent FDMI	Section I, Question 4
--today	Section I, Question 4.1
	Section I, Question 4.2
E. Financial Criteria:	
--most recent FDMI	Section I, Question 5
--today	Section I, Question 5.1
	Section I, Question 5.2
F. Income Measure:	
--most recent FDMI	Section I, Question 6
--today	Section I, Question 6.1
	Section I, Question 6.2

Table 4 (Continued)

Variable	Information Source (Section, Question, Part)
G. Investment Measure:	
--most recent FDMI	Section I, Question 7
--today	Section I, Question 7.1
	Section I, Question 7.2
H. Cost of Capital:	
--most recent FDMI	Section I, Question 8
--today	Section I, Question 8.1
	Section I, Question 8.2

their investment evaluation process the unique risks inherent in international investments, i.e., foreign currency and political risks. This information was then tested for relationships with the demographic variables and with the motives and objectives of investment.

Additional information sought in this section of the questionnaire included the perceived riskiness of the environment for companies' most recent FDMI and the actual loss record of companies due to changes in the foreign currency and political environments in which they operate. Data on these variables were used in conjunction with those on risk analysis methods to test hypotheses from the behavioral theory. (Table 5 provides a list of the variables and corresponding questions from Section II of the questionnaire.)

The fourth and final section of the questionnaire, Comments, was designed to elicit open-ended replies from the respondents. The comments focused on changes in corporate practices regarding international investment decisions over time, differences between foreign and domestic evaluation practices, and perceived problem areas in the future. The responses to these questions provided greater perspective on the survey results and were used in combination with other key questions to select companies for the follow-up field work. (Table 6 provides a list of the variables and corresponding questions from Section IV of the questionnaire.)

The Field Study

The second stage of this research involved the selection and contacting of firms to participate in the follow-up interviews. The purpose of these interviews was to explore particular responses to the survey more completely in order to gain a better understanding of the relationships between variables. Specifically, the field study sought to:

1. Highlight the sensitivity of evaluation methods to environmental differences overseas.
2. Highlight the importance of organizational and operating factors in explaining the evaluation measures used.
3. Gain insight into the flow of information in the foreign investment decision process.
4. Gain insight into why companies selected certain practices over others.
5. Gain a greater understanding of the differences between foreign and domestic evaluation practices.
6. Understand the obstacles companies face in developing and adopting more sophisticated evaluation methods.

Table 5

Survey Source of Risk Analysis Methods

Variable	Information Source (Section, Question, Part)
III. Risk Analysis Methods	
A. Perceived Riskiness of Most Recent FDMI	Section II, Question 1
B. Business Risk Measure:	
--most recent FDMI	Section II, Question 2
--today	Section II, Question 2.1
	Section II, Question 2.2
C. Adjustments for Business Risk:	
--most recent FDMI	Section II, Question 3
--today	Section II, Question 3.1
	Section II, Question 3.2
D. Political Risk Definition:	
--most recent FDMI	Section II, Question 4
--today	Section II, Question 4.1
	Section II, Question 4.2
E. Political Risk Measure:	
--most recent FDMI	Section II, Question 5
--today	Section II, Question 5.1
	Section II, Question 5.2
F. Adjustment for Political Risk:	
--most recent FDMI	Section II, Question 6
--today	Section II, Question 6.1
	Section II, Question 6.2

Table 5 (Continued)

Variable	Information Source (Section, Question, Part)
G. Currency for Evaluating Investment:	
--most recent FDMI	Section II, Question 7
--today	Section II, Question 7.1
	Section II, Question 7.2
H. Foreign Currency (FC) Risk Definition:	
--most recent FDMI	Section II, Question 8
--today	Section II, Question 8.1
	Section II, Question 8.2
I. Measure of FC Risk:	
--most recent FDMI	Section II, Question 9
--today	Section II, Question 9.1
	Section II, Question 9.2
J. Adjustments for FC Risk:	
--most recent FDMI	Section II, Question 10
--today	Section II, Question 10.1
	Section II, Question 10.2
K. Impact of Foreign Risks	Section II, Question 11

Table 6

Survey Source of Respondents' Comments

Variable	Information Source (Section, Question, Part)
IV. Changes in Practices	
A. Reason for Differences in Practices Between Most Recent FDMI and Today	Section IV, Question 1
B. Reason for Differences in Domestic Versus Foreign Practice	Section IV, Question 2
C. Changes in Practices Over Time	Section IV, Question 3
D. Satisfaction with Present Practices	Section IV, Question 4
E. Obstacles to Improving Practices	Section IV, Question 5

A list of the questions covered in the field interview is included in Appendix C.

Twenty-five firms, nearly a quarter of the survey respondents, participated in the follow-up interviews. Fifteen were contacted by telephone in interviews lasting from one-half hour to two hours. The average telephone interview lasted about 45 minutes. Ten companies were interviewed by personal visits lasting from one to four hours. In several cases during these visits, more than one corporate executive was interviewed. For example, at one company the manager of foreign exchange, the director of corporate development, the chief financial officer, and the head of internal controls were all interviewed, providing a broad insight into organizational interaction in the foreign investment decision.

The companies contacted for the field study were selected on the basis of their responses to certain questions in the survey. Answers to questions 5 and 8 in Section I, 2, 3, 7, and 11 in Section II, and 1 and 2 in Section IV were the key discriminators. Companies tended to use similar measures and adjustments to capture business, political, and foreign currency risks so that questions 2 and 3 in Section II were used as proxies for 5, 6, 9, and 10 in Section II. As Katz points out (in contrast to a survey), "a field study is more concerned with a thorough account of the processes under investigation than with their typicality in a larger universe" (1953, p. 57). The same holds true for this research. Rather than striving to reflect the characteristics of the entire sample, selection criteria for the interviews sought to enable the researcher to explore in depth a diversity of evaluation practices and risk analysis methods.

Anticipated Results

The anticipated results described in this section derive from two main sources: earlier research in the area of financial and capital-budgeting practices of MNCs and the behavioral theory of corporate decision-making. These expectations are tempered by personal experience. One of the pioneering investigations into financial practices of MNCs was conducted in the later 1960s by Robbins and Stobaugh (1973) as part of the Multinational Enterprise Study at Harvard. They postulated eight variables to explain behavior of multinational enterprises: (1) foreign sales, (2) number of years since the first manufacturing facility was established abroad, (3) number of countries in which the enterprise manufactures, (4) average sales in each foreign country in which the enterprise manufactures, (5) foreign sales as a percentage of total sales, (6) total sales of the enterprise, (7) percentage of subsidiaries wholly owned, and (8) technology level of the firm. Through the use of factor analysis they found that the first variable—size of foreign sales—could be used as a proxy for the first six variables. Using a cross-tabulation table with a chi-square significance test, they determined that financial practices of MNCs were more often correlated with foreign sales than with either of the other two independent variables.

Along this line, it was expected that size would be a key discriminator of FDMI practices. Size was measured in terms of total and foreign sales, assets, and income. Foreign sales was anticipated to be related to the other variables and was expected to be the most important explanatory variable of the six. Large firms should use more sophisticated evaluation practices than small firms. Sophisticated practices include comparative evaluation of investment opportunities, use of net present value investment criteria, use of discounted cash-flow income measures, use of a weighted average cost of capital, and evaluation of investment opportunities in terms of both dollars and local currencies.

Large companies were also expected to use different risk analysis methods than small companies. Large companies should use sophisticated methods such as the use of probability distributions of cash flows, covariance of cash flows with other project cash flows or sensitivity analysis of cash flows to measure overall risk, foreign currency risk and political risk; the use of present and future cash flows to assess foreign currency risk; and the use of capital-budgeting procedures that adjust for the unique risks of international operations.

In addition to size, several other explanatory variables were postulated: *age* of a firm as a multinational, the *importance of a company's foreign operations* (i.e., foreign sales/total sales, foreign assets/total assets, foreign income/total income), the *geographic distribution* of a firm's foreign operations (the number of areas worldwide in which a firm has a FDMI), and the *extensiveness* of a firm's foreign involvement (the number of countries worldwide in which a firm has a FDMI). Old multinationals having greater experience at operating internationally were expected to have developed more sophisticated investment evaluation and risk analysis methods. In companies where foreign operations are an important contributor to total corporate performance, it was expected that more management attention and resources would have been devoted to developing sophisticated investment evaluation and risk analysis practices. The same expectation held for companies with extensive and widely dispersed overseas operations.

The anticipated findings described so far relate to relationships between demographic variables and companies' investment evaluation and risk analysis practices. Based on the behavioral theory of firm decision-making, several other results were anticipated. First, the behavioral theory postulates that firms seek to satisfy multiple objectives (as opposed to a single profit-maximizing goal of traditional theory). Thus, it was expected that FDMI evaluation will be subject to several objectives.

Second, Aharoni (1966) found in his investigations of foreign investment decision behavior that the decision-maker strongly influenced the type and scope of investigation into an investment opportunity. Thus, it was anticipated that the decision-maker's level in the firm would be an important discriminatory variable. Consistent with Aharoni's findings, it was expected that the higher up in the corporate structure the decision-maker is, the more sophisticated the evaluation procedures and risk analysis methods employed. Also, for cases where the decision-maker for the most recent FDMI differs from the decision-maker today, evaluation and risk analysis practices should differ as well.

Third, the behavioral theory emphasizes that the firm is a coalition of subgroups (rather than a single unit with one goal). Thus, the behavioral theory approach views the organizational structure of a company as a key variable in the analysis of firm decision-making. How companies are organized globally was expected to help explain the type of investment evaluation and risk analysis methods they employ. Davis (1976) has described the evolution of multinational corporate organization as moving from no international organization, to international division, to either a geographic product or functional organization internationally, to, finally, a matrix structure. It was expected that companies exhibiting a matrix or geographic, functional, product organization would employ sophisticated techniques for investment evaluation and risk analysis, while companies with no international organization or an international division would use less sophisticated techniques.

Fourth, according to the behavioral theory, search for the solution to a problem is limited. Aharoni (1966), Carter (1969), and Clarkson (1962) have all found that decision behavior is not characterized by a search for the "best" solution. Rather, search is made to find the first feasible alternative to solve a problem. Thus, it was expected that corporate behavior with respect to FDMI evaluation would be characterized by go-no go decisions on specific opportunities rather than comparative analysis.

Not only is search limited, it is also biased. Aharoni (1966) found that how a problem is defined affects the factors considered in seeking a solution. Thus, problem definition (in this research, the motive for investing overseas) was expected to be related to the evaluation methods employed for analyzing a specific FDMI.

Finally, the behavioral theory postulates that decision-making is characterized by uncertainty avoidance. Cyert and March (1959) found that corporations sought to avoid risk in decision-making by following industry tradition. It was expected that companies in the same industry would use similar investment evaluation and risk analysis methods. Further, Carter (1969) found that the more uncertain the environment, the greater the number of criteria an investment was evaluated on. It was expected that companies whose most recent FDMI was made outside the industry of the parent would subject that decision to a greater number of and more sophisticated evaluation methods than companies who invest overseas in their own industry.

Cyert and March (1962) also found that companies seek to avoid uncertainty in decision-making by utilizing standard operating procedures. This implies that standard procedures would be used to evaluate investment opportunities worldwide. It was expected that any changes noted in FDMI evaluation practices should be due to changes in practices over time, rather than changes to reflect specific characteristics of the investment opportunity (geographic area, etc.). However, the behavioral theory also stresses that organizations learn. Through experience, firms learn what aspects of the environment to pay attention to. So the expected result stated above applied only to the subgroup of companies that have not experienced foreign currency or politically related losses in the past 10 years. Companies with foreign currency losses were expected to use sophisticated foreign currency risk assessment methods. Companies with losses due to changes in the political environment should use sophisticated political risk assessment techniques.

Finally, based on personal experience, it was expected that the overall decision behavior of MNCs would more closely parallel that described by the behavioral theory than by the traditional economic view of firm decision-making. With specific reference to the generally received normative theory of international investment analysis (see Bavishi, 1979), based on the economic model, it was felt that actual corporate behavior would differ from the model's prescriptions in the area of risk evaluation and adjustments.

The anticipated outcomes of this research have been derived from a combination of prior research, theory, and personal experience. How closely the actual results correspond to expectations was discovered via the analysis described in the next section.

Analysis of Results

As a first step in organizing the results of this research, correlation analysis was undertaken on the demographic information received from the questionnaire. This analysis was run on information characterizing the respondent companies at the time of their most recent FDMI and today. The purpose of the correlation investigation was to determine if certain variables could be used as proxies for a larger group of demographic variables in the subsequent analysis of the power of these variables in explaining differences between companies in terms of the investment evaluation practices and risk analysis methods. For example, the correlation analysis was used to determine if, as Robbin and Stobaugh found, foreign sales could be used as a proxy for several other measures of foreign involvement. If so, foreign sales would be used as an independent variable in analyzing investment evaluation and risk analysis practices, and the correlated variables would not be used.

Next, frequency tables were developed for each of the eight investment evaluation practices variables. These tables were constructed for practices at the time of the most recent FDMI and today. Frequencies were calculated on which practices companies employed, and also the number of practices for each variable companies used. The tables were compiled for the sample overall and for various subgroups of the important demographic variables. This analysis enabled comparisons of actual to theoretically prescribed evaluation practices.

An analysis using a cross-tabulation table with a chi-square significance test was performed for each of the demographic explanatory variables with each dependent evaluation practice variable. These analyses were conducted by matching explanatory variables at the time of the most recent FDMI to dependent variables at that time and then repeated by matching explanatory variables as of today with dependent variables today.

A similar procedure was followed to analyze corporate risk analysis methods. Frequency tables were constructed and a cross-tabulation analysis undertaken. The chi-square measure was used to test for significance. An α level of .05 was used as the criterion for statistical significance in all the tests reported.

In order to test for significant changes in practices between the time of the most recent FDMI and today, the number of changes for each company was calculated. Paired t-tests were conducted on the responses to each evaluation practice.

In order to explore the congruence of the survey results with the results anticipated on the basis of the behavioral theory of firm decision-making, the following analyses were undertaken. First, the number of firms subjecting FDMI decisions to multiple objectives was tested for statistically significant difference-from-chance occurrence. This test was conducted on the basis of the most recent FDMI and today for the sample as a whole, using the chi-square test.

Next, several analyses were undertaken to explore the relationship of the decision-maker to risk analysis methods and investment evaluation practices employed. The cross-tabulation table with chi-square significance test was used to assess the relationship between the decision-maker and the type of practices and measures used.

An analysis of the relationship between organizational structure and the investment evaluation practices and risk analysis methods of companies at the time of most recent FDMI and today was carried out along the lines of that described for the general demographic variables.

Next, the number of firms using comparative methods of investment evaluation was tested for significant difference-from-chance occurrence using the chi-square test. This test was conducted for the sample as a whole and for demographic subgroups.

The relationship between motive for a FDMI and investment evaluation practice and risk analysis method was explored. These analyses used cross-tabulation with a chi-square significance test.

Within the general demographic analysis, specific attention was given to investigating whether companies within an industry used similar investment evaluation practices and risk analysis methods. Similarly, the practices of companies making a FDMI outside their own industry were compared with those investing in the same industry as the parent. This analysis was conducted only for the most recent FDMI.

Finally, the FDMI evaluation practices and risk analysis methods of companies which suffered foreign currency or politically related losses were compared with those of companies without losses. This analysis was done on the basis of practices today and encompassed the type of practices a company used for each dependent variable. A cross-tabulation table with chi-square significance test was used.

The last stage of the analysis was the organization and tabulation of responses to the personal and telephone interviews. Frequency tables were constructed for each of the risk analysis and investment evaluation variables. A description of the organizational context of the decision for each firm was written as well as an in-depth explanation as to why certain approaches were followed and alternatives were not.

Overall, analysis of the results of this research employed standard statistical procedures: frequency tables, cross-tabulation tables, chi-square tests of significance, and paired t-tests. These statistical methods met the research objectives of discovering if significant relationships exist between variables and testing broad hypotheses drawn from the behavioral theory of corporate decision-making.

Summary

The methodology used here is consistent with the specific goals of the research which are to:

1. Document the international investment motives and evaluation practices of U.S.-based MNCs.
2. Discover significant variables and relationships between variables in the international investment decision process of MNCs.
3. Test broad hypotheses on international investment decision-making drawn from the behavioral theory framework.

A mail questionnaire sent to a sample of 255 U.S.-based manufacturing MNCs in conjunction with a field study were the research methods utilized. The methodology was designed to take advantage of the strengths of each research approach while reducing, where possible, its weaknesses.

Drawing on earlier research, theory, and personal experience, the results anticipated from the research have been specified. Standard statistical procedures have been used to analyze the actual results of the study. These procedures were selected because they are widely understood and because they are congruent with the research objectives. The results of the research are detailed in the next chapter.

6

Results

Overview

The results analyzed and discussed in this chapter represent a combination of the tabulated responses to the questionnaire and explanations of the additional information collected through personal and telephone interviews with executives of the participating MNCs. The chapter is organized to parallel the objectives of the research. First is a discussion of the characteristics of the survey respondents. Next follows a documentation of the foreign investment evaluation practices of the sample firms. This section employs frequency distributions and paired t-tests as the main method of analysis.

The third section contains statistical analysis of the relationships of demographic and organizational variables to foreign evaluation practices. Cross-tabulation tables with chi-square analysis are the primary methods used in this section. An α level of .05 is used as the criterion for statistical significance in all of the tests reported.

Throughout the first three sections, comments from the personal and telephone interviews are included when they clarify the documented responses or relationships. The majority of this information is presented as a separate and final section of this chapter.

The results discussed in the next four sections of this chapter are based on 108 completed mail questionnaires and 25 telephone and personal interviews. Out of 225 questionnaires mailed, 155 companies responded for an overall response rate of 60.8 percent. Of these, 27 said that they did not qualify as manufacturing MNCs and 20 refused for various reasons to complete the survey. Each of the remaining 100 companies that did not respond to the follow-up request for participation was contacted by telephone. Twenty-six of these companies did not qualify as manufacturing MNCs, leaving an eligible sample of 202. The 108 completed surveys represent α 53.5 percent response rate from the eligible firms.

This response rate reflects favorably with those from other similar research efforts. In a 1979 study of international performance evaluation practices, Morsicato obtained a 38.5 percent response rate from a mail questionnaire to 293 chemical companies. McInnes (1971) received a 30 percent response to his mail survey of international financial reporting practices of 100 U.S.-based companies. Two recent surveys of domestic capital-budgeting practices, one by Klammer (1972) and one by Schall et al. (1978), received 49.9 and 46.4 percent responses, respectively. And an earlier study of international capital-budgeting practices by Stonehill and Nathanson (1968) achieved a 42.0 percent response rate. The positive response to the present survey is due not only to the steps detailed in the methodology chapter but also to the high level of interest the topic holds for corporate executives today.

The current importance of the topic is further attested to by the willingness of the respondents to participate further in the telephone and personal interviews. Not one company selected for the field study refused to participate. An analysis of the characteristics of the total sample follows, while a discussion of the field study sample is reserved for the final section of this chapter.

Characteristics of Responding Firms

A total of 108 firms responded to the mail questionnaire. Only 105 of these responses enter into the tabulated responses which form the basis for the statistical analyses presented in this chapter. Three questionnaires were returned too late to be included in the statistical analysis.

As expected from the definition used to select companies for the study, the group consisted of large, geographically diversified companies which have been MNCs for some time. Table 7 presents a financial profile[1] of the respondent companies. Mean total sales for the group in 1978 equaled $5,767 million, with a range of $408 million to $42,784 million. The sample had average assets of $3,680 million, ranging from $330 million to $22,101 million, and average operating income of $403 million, with a range of $0 to $1,589 million.

The companies were heavily committed to foreign operations. On average they achieved 30.4 percent of their total sales from foreign sales, they held 29.1 percent of their assets overseas, and they derived 28.0 percent of their operating income from foreign sources. In addition, these firms have had a long-term commitment to foreign involvement. As Table 8 indicates, 84 percent of the companies have been MNCs for the past 10 years and nearly 44 percent have been since 1960.

The companies had a widespread geographic commitment overseas. Table 9 presents the frequency analysis of the number of different areas the

Table 7

Financial Profile of Sample Companies

At the Time of Most Recent FDMI (Mean[a])	Today (Mean)	Financial Performance
5,281	5,767	Gross sales for the total company (million $)
30.7	30.4	Percent of total gross sales from foreign operations
2,400	3,680	Total company identifiable assets (million $)
28.1	29.1	Percent of identifiable assets in foreign operations
381	403	Total company operating income (million $)
29.0	28.0	Percent of total operating income from foreign operations

[a] These figures represent the mean values for the various financial variables for the 105 companies.

Table 8

Age as a Multinational of Companies in the Sample

Companies Qualifying as a Multinational (Percent[a])	Year
100.0	1978
83.8	1970
43.8	1960
20.0	1950

[a] These figures represent the percent of the 105 firms which reported qualifying as a manufacturing MNC in the four years 1978, 1970, 1960, 1950.

Table 9

Geographic Dispersion of Investment for Sample Companies

Relative Frequency (Percent)	Number of Different Geographic Areas a Company Has Investments In
0.0	0
0.0	1
1.0	2
16.2	3
21.9	4
40.0	5
15.2	6
5.7	7

sample companies operate in overseas. The possible areas included Europe, the Middle East, Africa, Asia and the Far East, Latin America, Canada, and "other." Nearly 83 percent of the companies had investments in four or more different areas. On average, the sample companies invested in six different countries in Europe, one each in the Middle East and Africa, three each in Asia and the Far East and Latin America, one in Canada, and four in the "other" categories (usually in Australia and New Zealand).

The pattern of where the sample companies had chosen to locate their most recent foreign direct manufacturing investment (FDMI) paralleled the current distribution of investments. As Table 10 indicates, by far the favorite area for investment was Europe, followed by Latin America and then by Asia and the Far East.

In terms of industry distribution of the sample, nine separate industry groups were represented. Table 11 presents the primary industry of the parent MNC as well as the industries in which the firms made their most recent FDMI. The largest industry group represented was the chemical industry, comprising almost a quarter of the sample. Only 23 firms made a foreign investment outside of the parent company's primary industry, with the largest changes occurring between the machinery and electrical machinery categories.

In summary, the respondent companies were large, geographically dispersed firms with a long-term and continuing involvement in foreign operations. They tended to invest in geographic areas in which foreign involvement already exists and to expand overseas in industries they already know. The investment evaluation practices which might contribute to such a pattern are described in the next section.

Documentation of Foreign Investment Evaluation Practices

The results analyzed and discussed in this section are based primarily on the responses to Sections I and II of the questionnaire (see Appendix B). Comments from the telephone and personal interviews are provided where applicable. The statistical analyses consist of frequency distributions for 20 separate investment evaluation practices. All of the frequency analyses are presented both for the practices as of the company's most recent foreign direct manufacturing investment and for the company's practices today.

The section is divided into two parts corresponding to Sections I and II of the questionnaire. The first part documents the firm's general foreign investment analysis practices. The second part documents how the sample companies analyze the unique risks of foreign investments, specifically foreign currency and political risks.

Table 10

Geographic Area Where Companies Made Their Most Recent Foreign Investment

For Most Recent FDMI (Percent)	Geographic Area
42.9	Europe
1.9	Middle East
1.9	Africa
17.1	Asia and Far East
32.4	Latin America
1.9	Canada
1.9	Other

Table 11

Differences Between Industry of the Parent Company and Industry of Foreign Investment

Parent Company (Percent[a])	Most Recent FDMI (Percent)	Industry
11.4	10.5	Food Products
4.8	5.7	Paper and Allied Products
24.8	25.7	Chemicals and Allied Products
2.9	1.0	Rubber Products
10.5	8.6	Primary and Fabricated Metals
17.1	12.4	Machinery (except electric)
7.6	10.5	Electrical Machinery
8.6	8.6	Transportation Equipment
12.4	17.1	Other

[a] These figures represent the percent of the 105 companies which reported the parent company was in a particular industry and that they invested in each industry.

General Foreign Investment Evaluation Practices

The results presented here document the general practices that the sample companies used to evaluate foreign investment opportunities. They include such policies as the general objectives and specific reasons for making foreign investments; the organizational structure for foreign operations; the decision-maker for foreign investments, the amount of comparative analysis undertaken, the financial criteria used to evaluate foreign investments as well as the definitions of income, investment, and cost of capital employed in the analysis.

Frequency distributions on these practices are derived from responses to Section I of the questionnaire. Comments on why certain practices (as opposed to other options in the questionnaire) are used by the respondents are presented. These were obtained in the telephone and personal interviews.

When asked what the general objective was in undertaking their most recent FDMI, by far the majority of companies (74.3 percent) responded that increasing profits was a main goal. Even a larger percentage, 80 percent, reported that increasing profits is a goal of investing abroad today.

But profit is not the only objective of foreign investments. Of the firms investigated, 43.8 percent of the firms sought to increase market share with both their most recent FDMI and with a FDMI today. This finding lends support to the positive theories that explain foreign investment behavior in terms of oligopoly strategy. Nearly 50.0 percent of the firms invested overseas to meet growth objectives, which is consistent with Polk's findings in the early 1960s. These results are presented in Table 12.

From Table 12 it is also evident that the percentage of companies subjecting foreign investments to a particular objective remains fairly constant between most recent FDMI and today. The only significant change is the increased number of companies investing abroad to reduce production costs. Fifteen companies had this as an objective for their most recent FDMI, while 20 companies use foreign investments to meet this goal today.

The sample companies had multiple objectives both for their most recent FDMIs and a FDMI today. A total of 212 responses were made, indicating an average of two objectives were used per company. Overall, these findings lend support to the behavioral formulation of multiple objectives guiding corporate foreign investment decisions. Although profit is an important goal, it is only one of several, including growth and market share objectives. Also, the traditional view of the firm as a profit *maximizer* is not supported by the results of the field research which indicate that companies accept projects which meet certain profit, growth, etc. objectives. Thus, firm decisions appear to be more consistent with "satisficing" behavior of the behavioral theory than the optimizing behavior of traditional theory.

Table 12

General Objectives of Undertaking a Foreign Investment

For Most Recent FDMI[a] (Percent[b])	For FDMI Today (Percent)	Objective
43.8	43.8	Increase Market Share
51.4	49.5	Increase Growth
74.3	80.0	Increase Profits
14.3	19.0	Decrease Production Costs
9.5	9.5	Decrease Risk Through Geographic Diversification

[a]FDMI is foreign direct manufacturing investment.

[b]These figures represent the percent of the 105 firms which reported having each objective when making a foreign investment. Percentage will not total 100 since firms reported multiple objectives.

Table 13 presents the frequency distributions of specific reasons companies gave for making their most recent FDMIs and undertaking foreign investments today. No one reason dominated for either case, although attempting to overcome tariff barriers ranked first both for most recent FDMI and today. If the reasons are grouped according to whether they are aggressive versus defensive motives, three could be considered aggressive (lower wage costs, take advantage of government incentives, and export market potential), three defensive (respond to government pressures to produce locally, overcome tariff barriers, and fear of losing export market), and for two it is unclear whether they are defensive or aggressive (gain economies of scale, follow customer). The combined percent of companies having aggressive motives for foreign investments today was 54.3, and the percent having defensive reasons was 70.5. These results do not provide clearcut support for either scenario of foreign investment strategy. However, the results clearly do not support the contention of labor groups that foreign investments are made primarily to exploit cheap labor overseas.

The "other" response for this survey question was large, reflecting the wide diversity of reasons why companies seek foreign investments. The most common response in this category was that companies invested overseas in order to control raw materials necessary in production. Increasingly, respondents said they were investing overseas to obtain cheap energy. This result seems to imply that some firms seek production sites overseas where factor availability and costs are consistent with their accustomed production processes. Thus, energy scarcity in the future may result in a shift in other productive factors to energy-abundance countries.

The next two general corporate practices firms pursued in evaluating foreign investment regard the way in which they organize to manage foreign operations and investment decisions. Table 14 depicts the percentage of the 105 companies that are organized globally by either geographic divisions, functional areas, product lines, international division, or in a matrix structure. The most popular organizational structure was to operate internationally by product lines, and this type of organization was used by more companies today than when they made their most recent FDMI. Use of an international division or a geographic division was decreasing while matrix organizations[2] are growing slightly in usage. This result parallels Davis' analysis (1976) of the organizational changes MNCs undergo as they age and develop.

Although the sample firms use many different organizational structures for foreign operations, two clearcut decision-makers for foreign investment opportunities emerge from the survey responses. Both for their most recent FDMI and an investment today, 66.7 percent of the companies said that the Board of Directors made foreign investment decisions. In addition, 57.1 percent responded that the Chief Executive Officer (CEO) had decision

Table 13

Specific Reason for Making a Foreign Investment

For Most Recent FDMI (Percent)[a]	For FDMI Today (Percent)	Specific Reason
26.7	25.7	Gain Economies of Scale
13.3	11.4	Lower Wage Costs
19.0	24.8	Respond to Government Pressures to Produce Locally
21.0	24.8	Take Advantage of Government Incentives
27.6	31.4	Overcome Tariff Barriers
20.0	18.1	Follow Customer
8.6	14.3	Fear of Losing Export Market
20.0	18.1	Market Potential
16.2	20.0	Other

[a] These figures represent the percent of the 105 firms that reported having each of the particular reasons for making a foreign investment. Percents do not total 100 since firms reported more than one reason.

Table 14

Organization for International Operations

At the Time of the Most Recent FDMI (Percent[a])	Today (Percent)	Organizational Structure
21.0	19.0	Organized globally by geographic divisions
1.0	1.9	Organized globally by functional area (e.g., finance, marketing, etc.)
31.4	34.3	Organized globally by product lines or groups
24.8	21.9	Using international division for foreign operations
21.9	22.9	Matrix

[a]These figures represent the percent of the 105 companies responding that they were organized in a particular way for international operations. Companies using more than one type of organization were classified in the "matrix" category.

authority in their most recent FDMI while 62.9 percent said that the CEO had that responsibility today. Table 15 indicates that other executives have had decision authority for foreign investments but that they are far less common than the Board of Directors or CEO.

Table 15

Organizational Level Where Foreign Investment Decision Is Made

For Most Recent FDMI (Percent[a])	For FDMI Today (Percent)	Decision Maker
66.7	66.7	Board of Directors
57.1	62.9	CEO
19.0	19.0	CFO
17.1	16.2	Area Manager
3.8	5.7	Regional Staff
4.8	5.7	Local Staff
13.3	12.4	Other

[a]These figures represent the percent of the 105 firms which responded that each particular decision maker had responsibility for foreign investment decisions. Percents do not total 100 because firms reported multiple decision makers.

The questionnaire asked respondents to differentiate between which individuals in the company might initiate an investment proposal, make the investment decision, and approve that decision. Respondents were asked to answer who *actually made* the foreign investment decision. The field interviews indicated that in almost all foreign investments the Board of Directors had final approval, especially if the investment was over a specific dollar limit. This limit varied by company but usually was in the $2-4 million range. Typically, even when the Board of Directors' approval was required, the actual decision was made by the CEO. Thus, the questionnaire responses may somewhat overstate the role of the Board of Directors and understate the importance of the CEO in foreign investment decisions. (A more complete description of the organizational context of foreign investment decisions is presented in the field study section of this chapter.)

In order to determine how closely corporate foreign investment analysis parallels the assumptions of traditional theory, companies were asked about the type of comparative analysis that opportunities were subjected to. As Table 16 indicates, the overwhelming majority of firms analyzed each investment separately, making a go-no go decision. This result supports the

Table 16

Degree of Comparative Analysis Foreign Investments Undergo

For Most Recent FDMI (Percent)[a]	For FDMI Today (Percent)	Type of Comparison
77.1	71.4	Each investment is analyzed separately and a go-no go decision is made
6.7	7.6	An investment is compared with a limited number of alternatives in the same geographic area
8.6	8.6	An investment is compared with a limited number of alternatives of the same type in all geographic areas
19.0	21.9	All investments worldwide are compared
0.0	1.0	Other

[a]These figures represent the percent of the 105 firms which responded that they subject for investments to each type of comparison. Percents do not total 100 because firms responded that they used more than one type of comparison.

behavioral view of investment decision-making as opposed to the traditional model.

Several companies interviewed in the field study indicated that the limited amount of capital available to their firms was forcing them to do more worldwide comparative analysis. One company stated that they searched worldwide for financing, and considered these funds as a pool available to finance projects anywhere in the world. All projects were then ranked according to their projected rate of return and projects were accepted until available financings were fully used.

By far the more common approach was that described by many of the firms interviewed. Each project was analyzed individually according to one or more criteria. If the project met the criteria, financing alternatives were found either locally or domestically and the project was undertaken.

The noncomparative nature of investment analysis and acceptable-level decision bebavior indicated by the results of the present research is at odds with the traditional economic model of firm investment decisions. It is significant that the present research indicates, as found by Cyert and March (1962), that firms' decision processes result in underexploitating the environment. Specifically, noncomparative analysis would seem to result in a less than optimal allocation of resources at a macro level, i.e., between countries, as well as at a micro level, i.e., between competing demands within the firm.

The importance of various financial criteria in evaluating foreign alternatives is presented in Table 17. Companies were asked to rate each of the six financial criteria from 1 (not important) to 5 (very important). Return on investment measures, either Accounting Return on Investment or Internal Rate of Return, were the most commonly used financial measures being ranked very important (5) by 33 companies and 49 companies, respectively, as a criterion for evaluating foreign investments today.

Payback was the next most common measure, ranked (5) by 23 companies. In the field studies, many firms indicated that payback was used more often in the analysis of foreign investments than domestic investments. Making sure that the investment would be returned quickly was seen as a way of adjusting for political risks like potential expropriation or blockage of funds for repatriation. The relative importance of the other financial criteria remained fairly constant for domestic versus foreign investments according to answers obtained in the field study.

In this aspect of their foreign investment evaluation practices, the majority of MNCs have adopted the methods advocated in normative theory; i.e., they employ a discounted cash flow financial criterion. The preference by MNCs for IRR as opposed to NPV measures stems from the prior use of return on sales or accounting return on investment before adoption of DCF

Table 17

Difference Between Ratings of Importance of Financial Criteria for Most Recent FDMI and an FDMI Today

Financial Criteria	Rating				
	Not Important 1	2	Important 3	4	Very Important 5
Payback[a]					
Most Recent	20.0	9.5	21.9	26.7	21.9
Today	19.0	11.4	22.9	24.8	21.9
Accounting ROI[b]					
Most Recent	24.8	16.2	16.2	11.4	31.4
Today	23.8	17.1	14.3	13.3	31.4
Return on Sales					
Most Recent	54.3	14.3	14.3	10.5	6.7
Today	53.3	12.4	10.2	9.5	8.6
Internal Rate of Return					
Most Recent	29.5	6.7	6.7	14.3	41.9
Today	28.6	4.8	5.7	14.3	46.7

Table 17 (Continued)

Financial Criteria	Not Important 1	2	Important 3	4	Very Important 5
Net Present Value					
Most Recent	52.4	4.8	18.1	9.5	15.2
Today	50.5	5.7	16.2	14.3	13.3
Contribution to EPS[c]					
Most Recent	33.3	15.2	16.2	20.0	15.2
Today	32.4	13.3	16.2	20.0	18.1

[a]These figures represent the percent of the 105 companies which ranked the particular financial criteria 1 to 5.

[b]ROI is return on investment.

[c]EPS is earnings per share.

methods. The normative literature prefers use of NPV to IRR for reasons well discussed elsewhere (see Rodriquez and Carter, 1976; Weston and Sorge, 1972). In terms of the accept-reject decisions that MNCs make, IRR and NPV give consistent results and the limitations of IRR measures decrease in importance.

The widespread acceptance of the payback measure as an investment criterion is counter to the normative prescriptions. The prime theoretical drawback of payback is that it ignores cash flows after the payback period and thus biases decisions in favor of investments with large returns early in the project life, and so may bypass projects of higher profitability over the long term.

The use of payback much more often for overseas than for domestic investments implies that corporate resources may be misallocated away from projects with long-term prospects overseas. This is especially true for investment opportunities in LDCs where use of payback analysis is most common.

The next three general practices which firms used to analyze foreign investments regard how they defined potential income, size of investment, and, if used, cost of capital. These results are presented in Tables 18, 19, and 20, respectively.

The most common measure of income was all earnings of the affiliate after foreign taxes, and 53.3 percent of the companies used this measure to evaluate investments today. However, many companies used more than one measure, doing the analysis on a cash inflow to the parent company as well. Cash inflows to the parent after foreign and domestic taxes was the second most common measure, being used by 43.8 percent of the companies today. The field survey results indicated that in the final analysis the evaluation of a project from a parent company perspective (i.e., in terms of dollar cash flow back to the parent company) is the determinant of whether an investment is undertaken.

Paralleling this parent company emphasis was the measure used to estimate the amount of investment required for a foreign opportunity. Over half of the firms used parent net contributions (parent share of equity capital plus loans and advances) to measure investment (Table 19). The second most popular measure was affiliate total capital employed, used by 42.9 percent of the companies for investments today.

Similarly, the most common definition of the cost of capital was a parent company weighted average, used by half of the companies (Table 20). Answers from the field study indicated that this cost of capital was rarely used as a discount rate in discounted cash flow analysis. Rather, the cost of capital was used as a hurdle rate against which investments are evaluated. For most companies a basic hurdle rate applied for all investments, domestic or foreign.

Table 18

Measure Used to Estimate Potential Income from a Foreign Investment

For Most Recent FDMI (Percent)[a]	For FDMI Today (Percent)	Measure of Income
58.1	53.3	All earnings after foreign taxes
15.2	21.9	All earnings after foreign taxes available for repatriation
41.0	43.8	All cash inflows to parent after foreign and domestic taxes
31.4	35.2	All cash inflows to parent plus reinvested earnings adjusted for foreign and domestic taxes
6.7	6.7	All cash inflows to parent plus reinvested earnings adjusted for foreign taxes only
4.8	4.8	Other

[a] These figures represent the percent of the 105 firms which responded that they used each particular income measure. Percents do not total 100 because firms use more than one measure.

Table 19

Measure Used to Estimate Amount of Investment Required for a Foreign Opportunity

For Most Recent FDMI (Percent[a])	For FDMI Today (Percent)	Measure of Investment
16.2	17.1	Affiliate Total Assets
40.0	42.9	Affiliate Total Capital Employed
21.9	22.9	Affiliate Net Worth
51.4	52.4	Parent Net Contributions[b]
30.5	28.6	Purchase Price
9.5	9.5	Other

[a] These figures represent the percent of the 105 firms which responded that they used each measure of investment. Percents do not total 100 because firms used more than one measure.

[b] Parent net contribution is parent share of equity capital plus loans and advances.

Table 20

Definition of Cost of Capital Used to Evaluate

Foreign Investments

For Most Recent FDMI (Percent[a])	For FDMI Today (Percent)	Cost of Capital
		Parent:
4.8	5.7	Cost of Debt
7.6	7.6	Cost of Equity
50.5	50.5	Weighted Average
		Local:
7.6	7.6	Cost of Debt
5.7	5.7	Cost of Equity
21.9	22.9	Weighted Average
13.4	14.4	Other

[a] These figures represent the percent of the 105 companies which responded that they used the particular definitions of cost of capital. Percents do not equal 100 because companies used multiple definitions.

This rate derived loosely from the parent company weighted average cost of capital, and was adjusted subjectively to reflect various foreign risks. How this adjustment is accomplished is the subject of the next part of this section.

Only partial agreement with normative theory is indicated by the practices of MNCs in these three aspects of investment evaluation. First, normative theory suggests that evaluation can be undertaken using either the subsidiary or parent respective. If the subsidiary viewpoint is used the proper cash flow definition should assume unremitted earnings are reinvested locally and will be available to the parent eventually. The majority of companies used this measure. If the parent perspective is used only remittable earnings should be counted as cash flow. Only 2.9 percent of the companies used this measure with most companies considering all cash flows to the parent in the analysis. Use of this measure overstates cash flows in blocked currency countries and could misallocate resources toward such investments.

Stonehill and Nathanson advocate analyzing foreign investment opportunities from both a subsidiary and parent perspective in order to achieve proper resource allocation within the company as well as efficient use of resources in the host country. Many companies seem to pursue this approach. Although the cash flow definition differs from those supported in the normative literature, the measures of investment parallel that prescribed. A discrepancy arises again in the cost of capital used by MNCs. Half the companies used the prescribed parent worldwide weighted average cost of capital. But 22.9 percent use a local cost of capital, which would either benefit or penalize these projects depending on whether the local cost of capital was lower or higher than the parent's cost. Since local costs usually exceed the parent's weighted average, foreign projects would be penalized and resources diverted from them. Although these are important discrepancies from normative theory, more important is the manner in which the cost of capital is used to reflect risks in the international environment. This is discussed in the next section of this chapter.

International Risk Analysis Methods

The results presented here document how the sample MNCs analyzed the risks inherent in foreign investments, i.e., the business, foreign currency, and political risks. Specific attention is focused on how the firms defined and measured these risks as well as on what adjustments they made in their capital-budgeting procedure to reflect the risks.

Frequency distributions on these practices are derived from responses to Section II of the questionnaire. Comments on why specific practices were chosen by certain companies are also presented. These were obtained in the telephone and personal interviews.

When asked how they measured the general business risk (i.e., the commercial, competitive, etc. risks) for foreign investments, nearly 84 percent of the sample firms reported that they made a subjective evaluation of risk for their most recent FDMI. The same percentage of companies use a subjective evaluation to analyze foreign opportunities today. Table 21 contains the frequency distribution of methods the sample firms used to measure business risk.

Table 21 also indicates that nearly half the firms used some sort of sensitivity analysis to measure business risk. From the field study it was evident that many companies used sensitivity analysis in conjunction with subjective evaluation to measure business risk. The subjective evaluation determined what factors were critical to success with a given investment. Then a sensitivity analysis was performed on these key variables, most often price and volume estimates. The most common practice was to project a best case, worst case, and most likely case with the final analysis being done on the most likely estimate.

Table 21

Measure Used to Estimate Business Risk of a Foreign Investment

For Most Recent FDMI (Percent[a])	For FDMI Today (Percent)	Business Risk Measure
83.8	83.8	Make a subjective evaluation of risk
23.8	25.7	Project a probability distribution of cash flows
3.8	5.7	Estimate the covariance of cash flows with other investment cash flows
46.7	47.6	Perform a sensitivity analysis
7.6	10.5	Calculate the probability of loss
2.9	1.9	Make no risk assessment
2.9	3.8	Other

[a] These figures represent the percent of the 105 companies which responded that they used a particular measure of business risk. Percents do not equal 100 because companies used multiple measures.

Only a quarter of the sample companies extended the sensitivity analysis to include probability estimates on projected cash flows. Several companies stated in the field interviews that their preference for less quantitative risk measures (i.e., subjective evaluation and sensitivity analysis as opposed to probability distributions) stemmed from two sources. First, they felt that their information was inadequate to enable them to formulate accurate probability estimates and that probability distributions gave the impression of greater precision than was warranted. Second, they felt that leaving the analysis in a more qualitative form enabled top management to evaluate better the underlying assumptions of the analysis and to see the range of possible outcomes of a project.

Once the business risk of a project has been measured, there are several adjustments that might be made in a firm's capital-budgeting procedures to reflect risk. Table 22 presents a summary of the adjustments that the sample firms made to reflect business risk of foreign investments.

The most common adjustment was to vary the rate of return required from a foreign investment. Fifty-seven percent of the firms said that this adjustment was made in analyzing their most recent FDMI and 60 percent made this adjustment today. The use of this type of adjustment is consistent with the importance companies place on return on investment as a financial criterion for evaluating foreign investments.

The second most popular adjustment was to require a faster payback for risky investments. Of the sample companies, 28.6 percent made this adjustment. An adjustment that is growing in usage is varying the cost of capital used in DCF analysis, while the practice of making no adjustment for risk is decreasing in importance. Even so, 19 companies made no adjustment in their capital-budgeting procedures to reflect business risk in analyzing foreign investments today.

Answers obtained in the telephone and personal interviews indicated that the adjustments made to reflect business risks were highly subjective. First, since little comparative analysis was undertaken no standard adjustments existed for given levels of risk. Also, since most companies used either subjective methods or sensitivity analysis to measure business risks, it was difficult for them to relate the amount of business risk to specific amounts of adjustment. Even companies using a probability distribution to measure business risk did not directly relate the spread in the distribution to specific adjustment amounts.

The most common practice was to begin with a corporate standard hurdle rate and to subjectively adjust the required rate for the combined business, political, and foreign currency risks of the investment. The final determination of the appropriate required rate of return was generally made by the CEO, often after consultation and negotiation with many other

Table 22

Adjustment Made in Capital-Budgeting Procedures to Reflect Business Risk of a Foreign Investment

For Most Recent FDMI (Percent[a])	For FDMI Today (Percent)	Adjustment to Reflect Business Risk
57.1	60.0	Vary rate of return required from the FDMI
21.0	25.7	Vary cost of capital used in discounted cash flow analysis
28.6	28.6	Vary payback period required from the FDMI
1.9	2.9	Insure risks and charge cash flows for these costs
5.7	5.7	Charge cash flows for cost of insuring risks even if not taken
23.8	18.1	Make no adjustment for risk
7.6	8.6	Other

[a] These figures represent the percent of the 105 companies which responded that they used a particular adjustment for business risk. Percents do not total 100 because companies used more than one adjustment.

corporate executives, e.g., the CFO, product or area manager, etc.

A pattern similar to that just described for the treatment of foreign business risks by the sample firms held true for their treatment of political and foreign currency risks. Table 23 presents the factors that companies considered in defining political risk. The most important element of political risk was repatriation restrictions. This definition was used by 82.9 percent of the sample in analyzing their most recent FDMI and 86.7 percent today. Operational restrictions were considered by 70.5 percent of the companies for their most recent FDMI and are analyzed today by 74.3 percent. Complete loss of the investment due to expropriation as nationalization was an important part of political risk for 66.7 percent of the firms in their most recent FDMI and for 73.3 percent today.

During the field interviews companies were asked if their definition of political risk changed for investments in different parts of the world. Many companies commented that the possibilities of repatriation restrictions were important sources of risk everywhere. This was consistent with the parent-company perspective most firms took in evaluating foreign investments. Many firms made a distinction in their political risk definition between less developed countries (LDC) and developed countries (DC). They emphasized expropriation and breaches of agreements in LDCs and operating restriction in DCs.

In measuring political risk the sample firms relied on subjective evaluation even more than they did for measuring business risk. Table 24 shows that nearly 90 percent of the sample firms used subjective means to measure political risk. The next most common measure was to perform a sensitivity analysis, used by 19 percent of the firms. Although projecting a probability distribution of cash flows is only used by 15.2 percent of the companies today, it has grown the most of all measures in usage.

In the telephone and personal interviews it became evident that the most usual approach for evaluating a political risk was to include a qualitative description of the political environment in an investment proposal. This description sought to highlight the key political factors of importance for the success of a project. But only if a sensitivity analysis was specifically requested would it be incorporated into the formal project analysis. In general, most companies did not include a descriptive analysis of the political environment for investments in DCs but the description is standard practice for investments in LDCs.

Although many of the companies interviewed subscribed to outside sources which rank or rate countries in terms of political factors, usually no attempt was made to translate these rankings into specific adjustments in required performance for an investment. As indicated in Table 25, the most common adjustment in capital-budgeting procedures to reflect political risk

Table 23

Definition of Political Risk Used in Evaluating Foreign Investments

For Most Recent FDMI (Percent)[a]	For FDMI Today (Percent)	Definition of Political Risk
66.7	73.3	Expropriation or nationalization
82.9	86.7	Restrictions on repatriations to parent (e.g., dividends, royalties, capital, etc.)
70.5	74.3	Operational restrictions (e.g., ownership, employment policies, market share, etc.)
21.9	27.3	Breaches or unilaterial changes in contracts and agreements
35.2	40.0	Discrimination (e.g., excessive taxation, requiring special operating permits, etc.)
10.6	7.7	Other

[a] The figures represent the percent of the 105 companies which responded that they used a particular definition for political risk. Percents do not equal 100 because companies used more than one definition.

Table 24

Measure Used to Estimate Political Risk for a Foreign Investment

For Most Recent FDMI (Percent[a])	For FDMI Today (Percent)	Political Risk Measure
87.6	89.5	Make subjective evaluation of political risk
9.5	15.2	Project a probability distribution of cash flows
0.0	1.0	Estimate the covariance of cash flows with other investment cash flows
19.0	19.0	Perform a sensitivity analysis
7.6	10.5	Calculate the probability of loss
3.8	1.9	Make no political risk assessment
2.9	1.9	Other

[a] These figures represent the percent of the 105 companies which responded that they used a particular measure of political risk. Percents do not total 100 because companies used more than one measure.

Table 25

Adjustment Made in Capital-Budgeting Procedures to Reflect Political Risk of a Foreign Investment

For Most Recent FDMI (Percent[a])	For FDMI Today (Percent)	Adjustment for Political Risk
54.3	57.1	Vary rate of return required from the FDMI
15.2	19.0	Vary cost of capital used in discounted cash flow analysis
25.7	27.6	Vary payback period required from the FDMI
4.8	7.6	Insure political risks and charge cash flows for cost of insurance
1.0	3.8	Charge cash flows for cost of insuring political risks even if not taken
33.3	29.5	Make no adjustment for political risk
7.6	8.6	Other

[a]These figures represent the percent of the 105 companies which responded that they used a particular adjustment for political risk. Percents do not total 100 because companies used more than one adjustment.

was to vary the required rate of return. Of the companies, 54.3 percent made this adjustment in evaluating their most recent FDMI and 57.1 percent use it today. The adjustment process was similar to that described for business risk; i.e., the amount of the adjustment is a highly subjective evaluation.

Over a quarter of the sample firms indicated that they adjusted the required payback to reflect political risk. In the field interviews, a number of firms indicated that they felt that payback was an important criterion for evaluating investments in LDCs because a quick payback lessened exposure to risk.

Nearly a third of the sample firms made no adjustment for political risk. When questioned about this in the field study, firms most often gave one of two responses. One group of companies made no quantitative adjustment to reflect political risk, feeling that a qualitative approach provided more information for the decision-maker. The second group indicated that the degree of political risk acted as a basic screen and that projects where political risk was high or a key factor in success would not reach the formal project stage. Thus, no adjustment for political risk was necessary in the capital-budgeting procedures.

Table 26

Currency Used to Evaluate Foreign Investment

For Most Recent FDMI (Percent[a])	For FDMI Today (Percent)	Currency
41.0	39.0	Dollars
4.8	4.8	Local Currency
54.3	56.2	Both

[a]These figures represent the percent of the 105 companies which responded that they evaluated foreign investment opportunities in dollars, local currency, or both.

Table 26 presents the results of the first of four questions designed to document how the MNCs analyze foreign currency risk of foreign investments. Over half of the firms conducted their analysis of foreign opportunities in terms of both dollars and local currency. Consistent with the parent-company viewpoint used by most companies, only 4.8 percent evaluated investments solely in local currency. In the personal and telephone interviews the majority of companies said that although earnings or cash flow estimates were projected in local currency, the final evaluation was almost always made in dollars. Thus, the questionnaire may understate the importance of dollar analysis of foreign investments.

When asked how they defined foreign currency risk for a foreign investment, many companies indicated that they used two methods. One definition employed a cash flow basis, either affiliate cash flows or potential cash flows to the parent. A supplementary analysis considered the possible impact of currency rate changes on reported financial statements of the parent company. As seen in Table 27, an accounting definition of exposure was used today by 87.6 percent of the companies. For companies using an earnings measure of income from an investment, this definition was the primary one used. For companies using a cash flow measure of income, the accounting definition was used as a supplemental analysis.

Many companies indicated in the field interviews that this emphasis on accounting exposure was a direct result of FASB #8. They also felt that FASB #8 had made top management more aware of foreign currency risks, and as a result these risks were receiving greater attention in investment analysis.

However, the measurement of foreign currency risks remains highly subjective in most companies. Table 28 indicates that 70.5 percent of the firms make a subjective evaluation of foreign currency risk today. From the field study it appeared that most companies projected income estimates first in local currency. These estimates were then translated to dollars using either the current exchange rate or a projected exchange rate. The actual investment decision was then made in dollars.

The projected exchange rate, when employed, was usually a treasury department estimate of the most likely rate for the life of the project. Over a third of the firms performed some sort of a sensitivity analysis, usually based on a most favorable, most likely, and least favorable rate. These estimates usually came from the treasury function and represent their judgment based on internal and external information. The most common external advice came from parent company banks.

Reflecting the growing emphasis on foreign currency risk, two more quantitative measures are being used by an increasing number of firms. Of the companies, 21.0 percent project a probability distribution of cash flows today versus only 13.3 percent for their most recent FDMI. Of the companies, 18.1 percent calculate the probability of loss from currency movements in analyzing investments today as compared with only 12.4 percent for their most recent FDMIs.

As seen in Table 29, a smaller percentage of companies made formal adjustments in the capital-budgeting procedures to reflect foreign currency risk than for business or political risks. Almost half of the companies made an

Table 27

Definition of Foreign Currency Exposure Used in Evaluating Foreign Investment

For Most Recent FDMI (Percent[a])	For FDMI Today (Percent)	Foreign Currency Exposure
46.7	50.5	Accounting translation exposure (affiliate-exposed assets - affiliate-exposed liabilities according to FASB #8)
36.2	37.1	Accounting translation exposure plus affiliate transactions in foreign currencies
1.9	2.9	Present cash flows to affiliate in foreign currencies
25.7	30.5	Present and future cash flows to affiliate in foreign currency
3.8	3.8	Present cash flows to parent in foreign currency
31.4	36.2	Present and future cash flows to parent in foreign currency
10.5	14.3	Other

[a] These figures represent the percent of the 105 companies which responded that they used a particular definition of currency exposure. Percents do not total 100 because companies used more than one definition.

Table 28

Measure Used to Estimate Foreign Currency Risk in Evaluating Foreign Investment

For Most Recent FDMI (Percent[a])	For FDMI Today (Percent)	Foreign Currency Risk Measure
74.3	70.5	Make subjective evaluation of foreign currency risk
13.3	21.0	Project a probability distribution of cash flows
1.0	1.9	Estimate covariance of cash flows with other investment cash flows
32.4	36.2	Perform a sensitivity analysis
12.4	18.1	Calculate the probability of loss
2.9	2.9	Make no foreign currency risk assessment
10.2	10.2	Other

[a]These figures represent the percent of the 105 companies which responded that they used a particular method to measure foreign currency risk. Percents do not total 100 because companies used more than one measure.

Table 29

Adjustment Made in Capital-Budgeting Procedures to Reflect Foreign Currency Risk of a Foreign Investment

For Most Recent FDMI (Percent)[a]	For FDMI Today (Percent)	Adjustment for Foreign Currency Risk
48.6	49.5	Vary rate of return required from the FDMI
12.4	17.1	Vary cost of capital used in discounted cash flow analysis
23.8	25.7	Vary payback period required from the FDMI
6.7	7.6	Insure foreign currency risks and charge cash flow for the cost
2.9	5.7	Charge cash flows for cost of insuring foreign currency risks even if not taken
31.4	26.7	Make no adjustment for foreign currency risk
6.7	7.6	Other

[a] These figures represent the percent of the 105 companies which responded that they used a particular adjustment for foreign currency risk. Percents do not equal 100 because companies used more than one adjustment.

adjustment by altering the return required. Again, this adjustment tended to be subjective.

When asked about these adjustments during the telephone and personal interviews, most companies responded that they tended to deal with foreign currency risks through operating policies rather than via adjustments in capital-budgeting procedures. For example, options for pricing policies, financing options to reduce exposure, etc. would be qualitatively analyzed in the investment proposal. But no formal adjustment would be made to required performance of an investment.

Overall, the risk analysis methods employed by the sample of MNCs differ from those proposed in normative theory more than their general evaluation practices. First, the methods used to measure business, political, and foreign currency risks are not the management science techniques advocated in theory, with the exception of the limited use of sensitivity analysis. Instead, foreign risks tend to be measured subjectively from a combination of factual information from inside and outside sources and long-standing personal impressions based on broad categorizations such as LDC versus DC.

Second, the adjustments to reflect these risks are not the certainty equivalent adjustment to cash flows or the risk-adjusted discount rate prescribed by normative theory. Instead, risks are reflected by an arbitrary increase in the required rate of return or shortening of the payback period. This latter adjustment is used most often for projects in LDCs. The adjustments made to financial criteria are not standardized to reflect equivalent amounts of risk, in part because the measurement techniques do not lend themselves to comparisons of risks for various projects.

The use of these practices has important implications for the allocation of corporate resources. The noncomparative judgmental measurement of foreign risks often results in a corporate policy of requiring higher returns in LDCs than in DCs and so may result in the misallocation of resources away from projects in LDCs. The use of a short payback criterion to adjust for risks in LDCs may produce a similar result and also biases resource allocation away from projects with long-term profitability but low initial cash flows. The use of arbitrary adjustments to required returns to reflect risks by ignoring the time pattern of risks penalizes all cash flows for risks that may be years in the future. Thus, a project with, for example, a large potential for expropriation next year bears the same adjustment as one that faces expropriation in 20 years with a resultant misallocation of corporate resources. The foreign risk adjustments used by MNCs typically lump all risks together. This practice makes it difficult for companies to discern the specific sources of risks for individual projects and thus is not conducive to controlling the risks after a project is accepted. Finally, the prevalence of a financial statement definition of foreign currency risk results in noneconomic decisions well documented elsewhere.[3] The consideration of this exposure may provide important information in evaluating financing alternatives to reduce foreign currency risk but should not be the definition of risk in investment decision-making if resources are to be allocated efficiently.

Summary of Investment Evaluation and Risk Analysis Practices

To summarize the foreign investment evaluation practices documented here: first, most companies invested abroad to meet multiple objectives with increasing profits the most important. The key decision-makers for foreign investments were the Board of Directors and the CEO. The vast majority of companies evaluated each foreign opportunity independently with some measure of return on investment as the key financial criterion. The majority of companies measured potential income from a foreign investment in terms of earnings after foreign taxes, although cash inflows to the parent after all taxes run a close second in usage. The most commonly used measure of the amount of foreign investment required for a project was parent net contributions, with affiliate total capital employed second. Finally, a majority of companies defined the cost of capital in terms of a weighted average for the parent company.

The weighted average served as a hurdle rate which was subjectively adjusted to reflect the risks of foreign investments. The vast majority of companies made a subjective evaluation of business risk and nearly half performed a sensitivity analysis, usually on price and volume estimates. The majority of companies reflected this risk in the capital-budgeting procedures by subjectively adjusting the rate of return required for the investment. Most companies defined political risk in terms of the threat of expropriation, operational, and capital flow restrictions. The amount of political risk was measured subjectively or by performing a sensitivity analysis. The most common adjustment to reflect business risk was varying the required return, although varying payback was also an important method. Many companies defined exposure to foreign currency risk in both accounting and cash flow terms, with the accounting focus having top management emphasis since FASB #8. Subjective evaluation and sensitivity analysis were the most popular methods of measuring foreign currency risk. Companies tended to adjust for currency risk by exploring alternative operating policies rather than varying required performance for an investment.

Most companies stated that the practices they used to evaluate their most recent FDMI were basically the same as the practices they use today. A correlation analysis between the responses for the most recent FDMI and today was undertaken for each possible answer, a total of 87. The lowest correlation was .70, with all but three being above 80 percent. Paired t tests were also run for each pair of answers. At an α level of .05 only in 17 out of the 87 cases did the responses change significantly for practices, as of the most recent FDMI to today. The significant changes occurred in the definition of political and foreign currency risks and the measure of and adjustments for foreign currency risks. This bears out the field study results that indicate an increasing emphasis on the definition and measurement of foreign currency risk. Because of the high degree of correlation between the responses for the most recent FDMI and today, many of the relationships analyzed in the next section are conducted on the basis of response for today's practices.

Relationships of Demographic and Organizational Variables to Foreign Investment Evaluation Practices

This section presents the results of statistical analyses into the relationships of demographic and organizational variables to foreign investment evaluation practices. The goal of these analyses was to attempt to find relationships that might be pursued in future research to develop positive and predictive models of foreign investment behavior. Cross-tabulation tables with chi-square analysis is the primary statistical method used, and the analysis is based on the responses to the mail questionnaire. An α level of .05 is used as the criterion for statistical significance in all of the tests reported. Where appropriate, comments from the field interviews are included.

This section is organized into three parts. The first part describes the relationships between various demographic variables and foreign investment evaluation practices. The second part discusses the relationships between organizational variables and foreign investment evaluation practices with specific attention given to tests of hypotheses drawn from the behavioral theory of corporate decision-making. The final part presents a summary of the relationships.

Relationships: Demographic Variables to Evaluation Practices

The results presented here describe the relationships discovered between demographic variables and foreign investment evaluation practices. The demographic variable included: measures of firm size (e.g., total sales, foreign sales, total assets, foreign assets, total income, and foreign income); measures of firm commitment to overseas operations (e.g., percent of total sales, assets and income from overseas sources); measures of geographic dispersion (e.g., the number of countries a firm operates in, the number of different geographic areas a firm operates in); age as a MNC; industry; and area of investment. The investment evaluation practice included: financial criteria for investment;

measure of income; measure of investment; definition of cost of capital; measure and adjustment for business risk; definition, measure, and adjustment for political risk; currency; and definition, measure, and adjustment for foreign currency risk. (These variables correspond to the following questions in the questionnaire: Section I, questions 5, 6, 7, 8,; Section II, questions 2, 3, 4, 5, 6, 7, 8, 9, 10.)

Because the questionnaire was designed to elicit the maximum amount of information from respondents, more than one answer could be given to each question. So in the statistical analysis each possible response for each question had to be treated as a separate variable. Using question 7, Section I, as an example, the question asked how a company measures investment for foreign opportunities. The possible answers were: affiliate total assets, affiliate total capital employed, affiliate net worth, parent net contributions, purchase price, and "other." Thus, in the statistical analysis one question has six variables to be considered.

For each demographic and organizational variable, 93 cross-tabulations with evaluation variables were constructed. In all, over 4,000 cross-tabulations were run. The results of these analyses follow.

Following the approach used by Robbins and Stobaugh (1973), the first step in the analysis was to see if any one financial variable could be used as a proxy for the others in the analysis of relationships with evaluation practices. Multiple regression analyses were run for total sales, assets and income, and foreign sales assets and income. The multiple R and R-square for foreign sales with each of the other variables is presented in Table 30. Due to the large degree of relationship between foreign sales and the other financial variables, only foreign sales was used in the subsequent analysis.

Table 30

Correlation of Foreign Sales with Other Financial Variables

Multiple R	R Squared	Financial Variable
.95	.94	Foreign Assets
.89	.97	Foreign Income
.96	.92	Total Sales
.88	.97	Total Assets
.74	.97	Total Income

The sample companies were divided into three groups: large, medium, and small. The small group with foreign sales less than $250 million contained 36 companies and had average sales of $151 million. The medium group with foreign sales between $250 and $700 million contained 34 companies and had average sales of $484 million. The large-company group with foreign sales greater than $700 million contained 35 firms and had average sales of $1909 million.

As stated earlier, 93 cross-tabulations were run for each demographic variable. The chi-square tables are presented only for variables with statistically significant relationships. Out of the 93 analyses performed, size of the parent company showed a statistically significant relationship with only four evaluation variables.

Table 31 shows the cross-tabulation table for the three size groups and the rating of importance for accounting return on investment (ROI) as an evaluation criterion. The chi-square is 15.59 with a significance of .049. The large firms tend to rate accounting ROI low (a 1) and small firms tend to give accounting ROI higher importance, as was expected based on prior research indicating that larger firms tend to use more sophisticated evaluation methods. Cramer's V was calculated and it equaled .272. So, the degree of association between size of the parent and rating of importance for accounting ROI was not strong. Asymmetric lambda which measures the percentage of improvement in ability to predict the value of the dependent variable given knowledge of the value of the independent variable was calculated. With size the independent variable lambda equaled .134. Thus, size increases prediction of rating on accounting ROI by 13.4 percent.

Size did not show a statistically significant relationship with the ratings that firms gave to any other financial criteria for evaluating foreign investments. Nor did size have a significant relationship with either the measure of income or the investment firms used to analyze foreign opportunities.

Size did show a significant relationship with the use of local cost of debt as a measure of cost of capital in foreign investment evaluation. As Table 32 indicates, chi-square was 6.77 with a significance of .034. Large firms dominated in the use of local cost of debt, representing 75 percent of the firms selecting this definition of the cost of capital. This result reflects the fact that many large firms view their foreign operations as distinct operating units, while small firms view foreign units as part of an integrated system. However, Cramer's V equaled only .254, which was not a particularly strong association, and lambda equaled 0.00 when size was the independent variable. So size provided no help in predicting the use of local cost of debt as a definition of cost of capital.

Table 31

Relationship Between Firm Size and Rating of Accounting Return on Investment as Financial Criterion

Firm Size	Rating of Accounting ROI (Percent)					Total
	1 (Not Important)	2	3	4	5 (Very Important)	
Small	24.0[a]	44.4	33.3	28.6	39.4	34.3
Medium	20.0	22.2	53.3	57.1	27.3	32.4
Large	56.0	33.3	13.3	14.3	33.3	33.3
Total	23.8	17.1	14.3	13.3	31.4	100.0

Chi-Square = 15.59   Degrees of Freedom = 8   Significance: .049

[a] These figures represent the percent of the companies selecting each rating that are small, medium, or large companies.

Table 32

Relationship Between Firm Size and Local Cost of Debt as Measure of Cost of Capital in Investment Evaluation

Firm Size	Use of Local Cost of Debt		
	Not Use (Percent[a])	Use (Percent)	Total (Percent)
Small	36.0	0.0	34.3
Medium	33.0	20.0	32.4
Large	31.0	80.0	33.3
Total	95.2	4.8	100.0
Chi-Square = 6.77	2 Degrees of Freedom		Significance = .034

[a] N = 105.

No other statistically significant relationships existed between size and definition of the cost of capital used to evaluate foreign investment. No significant relationships were found between firm size and the measure of business risk, the adjustments made for business risk, or the definition of political risk. There was a significant realtionship between size and the measure used to evaluate political risk.

As Table 33 indicates, the small firms tended to dominate in the use of probability distributions of cash flows to measure political risk. This result is counter to that expected at the outset of the study, but may reflect the fact that small firms tend to view political risks as the most important risks in foreign investments and so tend to use the most sophisticated measures possible. Small firms represented 34.3 percent of the total sample, but 56.3 percent of the firms using probability distributions. The chi-square value was 6.73 with significance of .034. The Cramer V was again relatively low, equaling .253, and a lambda value of 0.00 with size the independent variable indicated a lack of predictive ability. Size did not exhibit a significant relationship with any other measures of political risk.

Size was significantly related to one of the possible adjustments for political risk, varying the rate of return required from the investment. Table 34 shows that the small firms tended to dominate in the use of this adjustment, representing 43.3 percent of the firms selecting this adjustment. The chi-square equaled 6.88 with significance of .032. Cramer's V was .256, and lambda with size the independent variable was .133, indicating a higher degree of association than in earlier relationships.

Size was not related to the other possible adjustments for political risk. Nor was size related significantly to the various foreign currency risk definitions, measures, or adjustments.

To summarize, size of the firm showed a statistically significant relationship to only four investment evaluation practices. Small firms tended to rate accounting ROI important as a financial criterion whereas large firms did not. Small firms did not use local cost of debt as a measure of the cost of capital. Large firms did. Small firms dominated in the use of probability distributions to measure political risk and in varying the rate of return required from an investment to adjust for political risk. For all of these relationships, measures of association (Cramer's V) and measures of predictive ability (lambda) were relatively low.

These findings differ from those of Robbins and Stobaugh (1973b). They found that firm size was a prime discriminator in the financing practices of MNCs. Firms size was not found to be such a discriminator of investment evaluation policies of MNCs. At the outset of the study it was anticipated that larger firms would use more sophisticated investment evaluation measures than smaller firms. This expectation was not borne out by the responses to the questionnaire.

Table 33

Relationship Between Firm Size and Use of Probability Distribution
of Cash Flows to Measure Political Risk

Firm Size	Not Use (Percent[a])	Use (Percent)	Total (Percent)
Small	30.3	56.3	34.3
Medium	37.1	6.3	32.4
Large	32.6	37.5	33.3
Total	84.8	15.2	100.0

Chi-Square = 6.73   2 Degrees of Freedom   Significance = .035

[a]N = 105.

Table 34

Relationship Between Firm Size and Use of Varied Rate of Return to Adjust for Political Risk

Firm Size	Use of Varied Rate of Return for Political Risk		
	Not Use (Percent[a])	Use (Percent)	Total (Percent)
Small	22.2	43.3	34.3
Medium	44.4	23.3	32.4
Large	33.3	33.3	33.3
Total	42.9	57.1	100.0

Chi-Square = 6.88   2 Degrees of Freedom   Significance = .032

[a] N = 105.

There are several possible reasons for this discrepancy of findings. One reason could be that all of the present sample might be thought of as large firms. However, the selection criterion for the present study was consistent with that used in the Robbins and Stobaugh research. Another reason may be the role of the decision-maker. In the Robbins and Stobaugh study the decision locus shifted in the various size groups, but it remained centralized in the present research. Finally certain characteristics of the type of decision may explain the differing results. Key to the importance of size in explaining financing behavior was the number of potential financial linkages, and this factor would not be important in the investment decision.

The second group of demographic variables have been tested for relationships with investment evaluation practices. These were the measures of overseas commitment (e.g., percent of total sales, assets, and income from foreign sources). However, since these variables correlated so highly with the size variable, foreign sales, a separate analysis was not undertaken for the commitment variables.

Again drawing on the Robbins and Stobaugh research, the third group of demographic variables tested was a measure of international geographic dispersion. This variable was measured in two ways: the number of different geographic areas companies invested in, and the number of different countries companies invested in. The two variables were highly correlated and so the measure of the number of different areas of investment was used in the statistical analysis. Two groups were formed from this variable: the high-dispersion group had investments in five or more different geographic areas; the low-dispersion group had investments in less than five areas.

Dispersion of investment had a statistically significant relationship with five of the 93 investment evaluation methods. Geographic area was not related to the importance of various financial criteria for evaluating foreign investments nor to the measure of income or investment.

Table 35 shows that companies with lower dispersion tended to favor parent weighted average definition of the cost of capital, which may reflect the relative ease of computing a weighted average when a more limited number of capital sources are available. These companies represent 39 percent of the total sample, but 49.1 percent of the companies using this definition of the cost of capital. The chi-square equaled 3.70 with significance at .055. The phi measure of association equaled .20 and lambda equaled .192 with dispersion the independent variable.

The remainder of the cost of capital definitions showed no significant relationship to dispersion. Nor did any of the business risk measures or adjustments. There was a significant relationship between dispersion and the consideration of operational restriction in defining political risk.

Table 36 shows that the high-dispersion group used this definition slightly more than the low-dispersion group. The chi-square was 5.15 with a significance of .023. The phi coefficient was .244, indicating a moderate amount of association between the two variables. However, dispersion was not a good predictor of the use of operational restrictions to define political risk. Lambda equaled 0.00.

Dispersion also showed a statistically significant relationship with descrimination as a definition of political risk. Table 37 shows the cross-tabulation table for these variables. The chi-square was 5.80 with significance of .016. Geographically dispersed companies tended to use this definition relatively more than less dispersed companies. Of the companies using this definition, 76.2 percent were in the high-dispersion group. The phi was .255. But, again, lambda equaled 0.00 when dispersion was the independent variable, indicating no predictive association. This finding reflects the results of the field study which indicates that firms with wide geographic dispersion stress the importance of coordinated activities worldwide and so tend to be sensitive to impediments to integrated operations.

Table 35

Relationship of Geographic Dispersion to Use of Parent Weighted Average Cost of Debt

Geographic Dispersion	Use of Parent Weighted Average Cost of Debt		
	Not Used (Percent[a])	Used (Percent)	Total (Percent)
Low	28.8	49.1	39.0
High	71.2	50.9	61.0
Total	49.5	50.5	100.0

Chi-Square = 3.70   1 Degree of Freedom   Significance = .055

[a] N = 105.

Table 36

Relationship of Geographic Dispersion to Use of Operational Restrictions to Define Political Risk

Geographic Dispersion	Use of Operational Restrictions to Define Political Risk		
	Not Used (Percent[a])	Used (Percent)	Total (Percent)
Low	59.3	32.1	39.0
High	40.7	67.9	61.0
Total	25.7	74.3	100.0

Chi-Square = 5.15   1 Degree of Freedom   Significance = .023

[a] N = 105.

Table 37

Relationship Between Geographic Dispersion and Use of Discrimination
to Define Political Risk

	Use of Discrimination to Define Political Risk		
Geographic Dispersion	Not Used (Percent[a])	Used (Percent)	Total (Percent)
Low	49.2	23.8	39.0
High	50.8	76.2	61.0
Total	60.0	40.0	100.0
Chi-Square = 5.80	1 Degree of Freedom		Significance = .016

[a] N = 105.

Table 38

Relationship of Geographic Dispersion to Use of Insuring
Political Risks

	Use of Insuring Political Risks		
Geographic Dispersion	Not Used (Percent[a])	Used (Percent)	Total (Percent)
Low	42.3	0.0	39.0
High	57.7	100.0	61.0
Total	92.4	7.6	100.0
Chi-Square = 3.91	1 Degree of Freedom		Significance = .048

[a] N = 105.

Dispersion showed no significant relationship to any other definition of political risk, nor to any of the measures of political risk. There was one significant relationship with an adjustment in capital-budgeting procedures to reflect political risk. Table 38 presents the cross-tabulation table between geographic dispersion and the practice of insuring for political risks and charging cash flows for these costs. This result is consistent with the fact that wide dispersion firms are particularly sensitive to political risks which interfere with coordinated worldwide operations. All of the firms following this practice were in the high-dispersion group. Chi-square was 3.91 with significance of .048. The phi coefficient was .230, indicating moderate strength of association between the variables. With dispersion the independent variable, lambda equaled 0.00.

Dispersion was not related to any other political risk adjustment. Nor was it related to the definition of foreign currency risk. Geographic dispersion was significantly related to the use of sensitivity analysis to measure foreign currency risk. It was not related to any other measure of foreign currency risk nor to any adjustment for foreign currency risk.

Table 39 presents the cross-tabulation table for the variables geographic dispersion and use of sensitivity analysis to measure foreign currency risk. The high-dispersion companies dominated, comprising 76.3 percent of the companies that used this measure. The chi-square equaled 4.94 with significance of .026. The phi coefficient was .237, and again the lambda was 0.00, with dispersion the independent variable.

In summary, low geographic dispersion showed a significant relationship with the use of parent weighted average cost of capital. High dispersion was related to the use of operational restrictions and discrimination in defining political risk. High dispersion was related to insuring political risks and charging cash flows for these costs. Finally high dispersion was related to the use of sensitivity analysis to measure foreign currency risks.

Although these five variables showed significant relationships to dispersion, the phi coefficients were relatively low at around 25 percent. The lambda measure of predictive ability was 0.00 for four of the variables, indicating that geographic dispersion was not a good predictor of evaluation practices of MNCs.

The next group of demographic variables tested for relationship with investment evaluation practices was the age of a company as a multinational. The companies were divided into four groups: multinational since 1978, 1970, 1960, or 1950. Cross-tabulations were then constructed for each evaluation practice. Four of these relationships proved significant.

Age as a MNC did not exhibit a statistically significant relationship with any of the definitions of income or investment. Nor did age show a significant relationship to the definition of the cost of capital except in the use of parent

Table 39

Relationship of Geographic Dispersion to Use of Sensitivity Analysis to Measure Foreign Currency Risk

	Use of Sensitivity Analysis		
Geographic Dispersion	Not Used (Percent[a])	Used (Percent)	Total (Percent)
Low	47.8	23.7	39.0
High	52.2	76.3	61.0
Total	63.8	36.2	100.0

Chi-Square = 4.74   1 Degree of Freedom   Significance = .026

[a]N = 105.

Table 40

Relationship Between Age and Use of Parent Weighted Average as a Definition of Cost of Capital

	Use of Parent Weighted Average Cost of Capital		
Multinational Since:	Not Used (Percent[a])	Used (Percent)	Total (Percent)
1978	25.0	7.5	16.2
1970	28.8	50.9	40.0
1960	21.2	26.4	23.8
1950	25.0	15.1	20.0
Total	49.5	50.5	100.0

Chi-Square = 9.74   3 Degrees of Freedom   Significance = .021

[a]N = 105.

weighted average cost of capital. A disproportionate percent of the companies using this measure were in the MNC since 1970 group. The new MNCs and old MNCs (since 1950) showed a disproportionately small usage of this definition. Table 40 depicts this relationship. The chi-square was 9.74 with significance of .021. Cramer's V showed a higher association than between other demographic variables and the evaluation measures at .304. With age as the independent variable, lambda equaled .269, indicating a fair predictive ability.

Age showed no significant relationship with the practices used to measure political risk. But age did exhibit a significant relationship with two of the possible adjustments that could be made to reflect business risk, varying the required rate of return and making no adjustment. As Table 41 indicates, of the firms using an adjustment to rate of return to reflect business risk, the firms that have been multinationals since 1970 showed a disproportionate use of the measure, while the 1960 group showed lower than expected usage. The chi-square was 10.08 with significance of .018. Cramer's V indicated a fair degree of association at .310, and asymmetric lambda was .167 with age the independent variable.

For no risk adjustment, the MNCs since 1970 and 1950 showed a less than proportionate usage, while those since 1978 and 1960 showed more. The chi-square was 15.48 with significance of .001. The Cramer V was the highest of all the variables tested so far, at .384, but the lambda with age independent was 0.00. (See Table 42.)

At the outset of the study it was anticipated that the older MNCs would use the more sophisticated investment evaluation practices. In this case it was expected that the younger two groups (1978 and 1970) would use no more risk adjustment than the older groups. The dichotomous results do not support this belief, and no theoretically based explanation for the result is readily available.[4] A possible area for future research would be to seek similarities in the foreign environments in the periods 1970 and 1950 versus 1960 and 1968 that might account for the dichotomous results.

Age showed a significant relationship with only one of the definitions of political risk, the "other" category. As Table 43 depicts, the companies in the 1960 group were 75 percent of the companies using this definition, but only 23.8 percent of the total sample. None of the older MNCs used this definition, and the two younger groups used it less than expected. The chi-square equaled 12.97 with significance of .005. Cramer's V measure of association was .352, but again lambda was 0.00. Age was not significant in relation to any of the remaining political or foreign currency risk analysis practices.

To summarize, age was significant in only 4 of 93 cross-tabulations with investment evaluation practices. Two of the significant relationships had fair-size Cramer V and lambda coefficients, but for two lambda was zero. It is possible that these were spurious relationships.

Table 41

Relationship Between Age and Use of Varied Rate of Return

as a Business Risk Adjustment

	Use of Varied Rate of Return as a Business Risk Adjustment		
Multinational Since:	Not Used (Percent[a])	Used (Percent)	Total (Percent)
1978	19.0	14.3	16.2
1970	26.2	49.2	40.0
1960	38.1	14.3	23.8
1950	16.7	22.2	20.0
Total	40.0	60.0	100.0

Chi-Square = 10.08   3 Degrees of Freedom   Significance = .018

[a]$N = 105$.

Table 42

Relationship Between Age and Use of No Risk Adjustment

for Business Risk

	Use of No Adjustment for Business Risk		
Multinational Since:	Not Used (Percent[a])	Used (Percent)	Total (Percent)
1978	14.0	26.3	16.2
1970	45.3	15.8	40.0
1960	17.4	52.6	23.8
1950	23.3	5.3	20.0
Total	81.9	18.1	100.0

Chi-Square = 15.48   3 Degrees of Freedom   Significance = .0014

[a]$N = 105$.

Table 43

Relationship Between Age and "Other" Definitions of Political Risk

	Use of "Other" Definitions of Political Risk		
Multinational Since:	Not Used (Percent[a])	Used (Percent)	Total (Percent)
1978	16.5	12.5	16.2
1970	42.3	12.5	40.0
1960	19.6	75.0	23.3
1950	21.6	0.0	20.0
Total	92.4	7.6	100.0

Chi-Square = 12.97   3 Degrees of Freedom   Significance = .005

[a] N = 105.

Based on earlier research of Horst (1972) and Caves (1974), the next set of demographic variables analyzed for relationship with the foreign investment evaluation practices was the industry of the parent and the industry of investment. Based on two-digit SIC codes, only a few companies in the sample invested outside their own industry. Thus, the analysis of relationships was conducted on the basis of the industry of investment and the dependent variables were evaluation methods for the companies' most recent FDMI.

Nine industry subgroups were formed (e.g., companies which invested in Foods versus those that did not, those investing in the Paper and Allied Products versus those that did not, etc.). Cross-tabulations were run for each group with each of the 93 evaluation variables for a total of 837 analyses. Out of these, only 11 significant relationships were found. Since these could be attributed to spurious relationships in the data, industry of investment did not appear to be an important explanatory variable of the investment evaluation practices used by MNCs.

Three other demographic variables that were tested resulted in no significant relationships with the investment evaluation practices. Absolute size of investment was used to create three equal groups. Small investment was

< $5 million, medium was $5-10 million, and large > $10 million. These groups showed a statistically significant relationship with three evaluation practices: use of affiliate total assets to define investment, use of parent weighted average as a cost of debt, and use of present and future cash flows to the parent as a definition of foreign currency risk. However, the Cramer V measures of association were around .25 and the lambdas were low to zero. Therefore, size of investment was not a good explanatory variable.

Percentage of ownership was used to create four groups based on the equity ownership that initial investment entailed: 1-24 percent, 25-50 percent, 51-99 percent, and 100 percent. It was expected that companies would evaluate minority investments differently than wholly owned operations due to differences in commitment, risk, and control. These groups were then used to test for relationship with the evaluation practices. Only one statistically significant relationship was found. Those companies that acquired a majority interest in an affiliate preferred a purchase price definition of investment, often because these companies were acquisitions. With one implicit relationship out of 93, ownership percentage is not a key explanatory variable of the evaluation practices of MNCs.

The last of the insignificant demographic variables tested was the method of investment that companies used for their most recent FDMIs. Two groups were formed: those companies investing via acquisition and those starting a new company. These groups were then tested for relationships with the investment evaluation practices. No significant relationships were found.

The last group of demographic variables tested was the area of investment for the companies' most recent FDMIs. Seven subgroups were created (e.g., invested in Europe versus not invested in Europe, invested in the Middle East versus not invested in the Middle East, etc.). Each group was then tested for relationships with the investment evaluation measures. The Europe versus Non-Europe, Asia versus Non-Asia, and Latin America versus Non-Latin America groups all exhibited significant relationships to the evaluation practices. The groups Africa versus Non-Africa, Middle East versus Non-Middle East, Canada versus Non-Canada, and "Other" versus Non-"Other" groups did not.

Investment in Latin America was the best discriminatory variable of the geographic groups, showing a statistically significant relationship with seven of the investment evaluation practices. It did not show a significant relationship with any of the measures of income or investment for a foreign opportunity. But investment in Latin America was significantly related to the use of a risk-free rate adjusted for risk as the cost of capital in foreign investment decisions. Based on results of the field research, this finding probably occurs because many firms investing in Latin America try to finance these investments locally as a means of reducing foreign currency exposure and so use the cost of this funding to evaluate investments.

As Table 44 shows, all of the companies using the risk-free rate also invested in Latin America. The chi-square was 4.26 with significance of .039. As was the case with many of the demographic variables, the phi coefficient was low at .201, and the asymmetric lambda with location of investment the independent variable was 0.00.

Investment in Latin America showed a significant relationship with two measures of business risk. Table 45 presents the cross-tabulation between investment in Latin America and the use of a probability distribution of cash flows to measure business risk. The companies that invested in Latin America used this measure less than expected. These companies represented 32.4 percent of the total sample but only 16.0 percent of the companies using probability distributions of cash flows. The chi-square was 4.02 with significance of .045. The phi coefficient was low at .196, and the lambda indicated no predictive ability with area of investment the independent variable.

Investment in Latin America also showed a significant relationship with the use of probability of loss to measure business risk. Table 46 shows that no companies investing in Latin America used this measure. The chi-square equaled 4.15 with significance of .042. As with the other relationships between investment in Latin America and evaluation practices, the phi coefficient of association is fairly low at .200, and the lambda was 0.00. The lack of use of these sophisticated measures probably reflects limitations imposed by relatively inadequate and unreliable information in Latin America which results in a reluctance to make probability estimates.

Investment in Latin America was significantly related to one adjustment for business risk, varying the cost of capital. Table 47 indicates that companies investing in Latin America use this adjustment more than expected. They represent 50 percent of the companies using this adjustment. The chi-square was 3.95 with .047 significance. The phi was low at .194, and lambda was 0.00 with investment in Latin America the independent variable. This finding is consistent with the use of a risk-adjusted local cost of capital by companies investing in Latin America.

Investment in Latin America did not exhibit a statistically significant relationship with any of the definitions of political risk, but it was related to the use of sensitivity analysis to measure political risk. As the cross-tabulations in Table 48 indicate, companies investing in Latin America used this measure more than expected from their representation in the sample. The companies represent 55 percent of the firms using sensitivity analysis to measure political risk. The chi-square for this relationship was 5.77 with significance of .016. The phi was higher than for the other Latin America relationships at .234. But the lambda was still 0.00.

Table 44

Relationship Between Investment in Latin America and Use of
Risk-Free Rate for the Cost of Capital

Area of Investment	Not Used (Percent[a])	Used (Percent)	Total (Percent)
	Use of Risk-Free Rate for Cost of Capital		
Latin America	31.1	100.0	67.6
Not Latin America	68.9	0.0	32.4
Total	98.1	1.9	100.0

Chi-Square = 4.26   1 Degree of Freedom   Significance = .039

[a] N = 105.

Table 45

Relationship Between Investment in Latin America and Use of
Probability Distributions to Measure Business Risk

Area of Investment	Not Used (Percent[a])	Used (Percent)	Total (Percent)
	Use of Probability Distributions to Measure Business Risk		
Latin America	37.5	16.0	32.4
Not Latin America	62.5	84.0	67.6
Total	76.2	23.8	100.0

[a] N = 105.

Table 46

Relationship of Investment in Latin America to Use of
Probability of Loss to Measure Business Risk

Area of Investment	Use of Probability Loss to Measure Business Risk		
	Not Used (Percent[a])	Used (Percent)	Total (Percent)
Latin America	64.9	0.0	32.4
Not Latin America	35.1	100.0	67.6
Total	92.4	7.6	100.0

[a]$N = 105$.

Table 47

Relationship Between Investment in Latin America and Use of
Varied Cost of Capital to Adjust for Business Risk

Area of Investment	Use of Varied Cost of Capital to Adjust for Business Risk		
	Not Used (Percent[a])	Used (Percent)	Total (Percent)
Latin America	27.7	50.0	32.4
Not Latin America	72.3	50.0	67.6
Total	79.0	21.0	100.0

[a]$N = 105$.

Table 48

Relationship Between Investment in Latin America and Use of
Sensitivity Analysis to Measure Political Risk

Area of Investment	Use of Sensitivity Analysis to Measure Political Risk		
	Not Used (Percent[a])	Used (Percent)	Total (Percent)
Latin America	27.1	55.0	32.4
Not Latin America	72.9	45.0	67.6
Total	81.0	19.0	100.0
Chi-Square = 5.77	1 Degree of Freedom		Significance = .016

[a] N = 105.

Table 49

Relationship Between Investment in Latin America and Use of
Varied Cost of Capital to Reflect Political Risk

Area of Investment	Use of Varied Cost of Capital to Reflect Political Risk		
	Not Used (Percent[a])	Used (Percent)	Total (Percent)
Latin America	28.1	56.3	32.4
Not Latin America	71.9	43.8	67.6
Total	84.8	15.2	100.0
Chi-Square = 4.91	1 Degree of Freedom		Significance = .026

[a] N = 105.

Similar to the use of a varied cost of capital to measure business risk, companies investing in Latin America used this adjustment to reflect political risk. Table 49 shows the cross-tabulations for this significant relationship. The chi-square was 4.91 with .027 significance. The association between the variables as measured by the phi coefficient was .216, but lambda was 0.00, indicating no predictive ability with area of investment the independent variable.

The only other significant relationship with investment in Latin America was the definition of foreign currency risk. It was not related to any measure or adjustment for foreign currency risk. Table 50 shows the cross-tabulation between investment in Latin America and the use of present and future cash flows to the affiliate in foreign currency as a definition of foreign currency risk. The chi-square equaled 6.52 with a .011 significance. Relatively few of the companies investing in Latin America used this definition. Due to the importance they place on currency risk in investments there, they focus on a parent perspective. The phi coefficient of .249 indicates a fairly strong association, but lambda remains 0.00.

To summarize, investment in Latin America showed a significant relationship with seven investment evaluation measures. Companies in Latin America tended to use a risk-free rate adjusted for risk as the cost of capital for foreign investment decisions. Consistent with this is the finding that these same companies varied the cost of capital to adjust for both business and political risks. These companies did not tend to use the relatively sophisticated measures of probability distributions of cash flows or probability of loss to measure business risk. They also made use of sensitivity analysis to measure political risk. These findings are consistent with the results of the field study that indicated companies considered investments in LDCs more uncertain than in DCs and so preferred sensitivity analysis to measure risk. The field study also indicated that companies investing in LDCs were particularly concerned with cash return to the parent. This is consistent with the finding that companies investing in Latin America do not use cash flows to the affiliate as a currency risk definition.

Investment in Asia and the Far East showed the next largest number of significant relationships with investment evaluation practices at five. First, companies investing in Asia tended to favor cash inflows to the parent after all taxes as a definition of income from foreign investments. Table 51 shows the cross-tabulations between the variables. The chi-square was 3.65 with significance of .050. Although the phi coefficient of .186 indicated a fairly low degree of association, there was some predictive ability with area of investment the independent variable. Lambda equaled .093.

Investment in Asia was not related to any of the definitions of investment for an overseas opportunity. However, it was significantly related to the use of

Table 50

Relationship Between Investment in Latin America and Use of
Present and Future Cash Flows to the Affiliate to
Define Currency Risk

	Use of Affiliate Cash Flows to Define Currency Risk		
Area of Investment	Not Used (Percent[a])	Used (Percent)	Total (Percent)
Latin America	40.3	15.2	32.4
Not Latin America	59.7	84.8	67.6
Total	68.6	31.4	100.0
Chi-Square = 6.52	1 Degree of Freedom		Significance = .011

[a] N = 105.

Table 51

Relationship Between Investment in Asia and Use of Cash Inflows
to the Parent to Define Income

	Use of Cash Inflows to Parent to Define Income		
Area of Investment	Not Used (Percent[a])	Used (Percent)	Total (Percent)
Asia and Far East	11.3	25.6	17.1
Not Asia and Far East	88.7	74.4	82.9
Total	59.0	41.0	100.0
Chi-Square = 3.65	1 Degree of Freedom		Significance = .050

[a] N = 105.

parent cost of debt as the cost of capital. Companies investing in Asia represented 60 percent of the companies using this measure of the cost of capital. The relationship presented in Table 52 has a chi-square of 6.79 with significance of .010. The phi coefficient is .254, but as with many of the relationships lambda was 0.00.

Investment in Asia and the Far East was also significantly related to the use of probability distribution of cash flows to measure business risk, possibly reflecting the greater availability and reliability of information on market competitive factors there than in Latin America. Thirty-two percent of the companies using this measure also invested in Asia. Companies investing in Asia represented only 17.1 percent of the total sample. Table 53 shows this relationship. The chi-square was 5.10 with .024 significance. The strength of association as measured by phi equaled .220, but lambda remained 0.00.

Investment in Asia and the Far East showed no significant relationships with any adjustment for business risk, with the definition, measurement, or adjustment for political risk, or the definition or measurement of foreign currency risk. It was significantly related to two adjustments for foreign currency risk.

Table 54 depicts the cross-tabulation between investment in Asia and use of a varied rate of return to adjust for foreign currency risk. Companies investing in Asia strongly preferred this adjustment. The relationship had a chi-square of 4.86 with significance of .027. The phi coefficient of .215 indicates a fairly strong association. Asymmetric lambda with investment in Asia independent was .157, indicating a better predictive ability than most relationships so far.

Finally, investment in Asia and the Far East was significantly related to one other foreign currency risk adjustment, the practice of not adjusting for currency risk. As Table 55 suggests, companies investing in Asia do not use this practice. Of the 33 companies not adjusting for currency risk, only two invested in Asia. The chi-square was 4.16 with .041 significance. Phi was .199, but lambda again equaled 0.00.

To summarize, investment in Asia and the Far East showed a significant relationship with five evaluation practices. Companies investing in Asia tended to take a strong parent-company perspective in foreign investment evaluation, using parent cash inflows to measure income and parent cost of debt as the cost of capital in investment evaluation. Companies investing in Asia tended to use the more sophisticated measure of business risk, a probability distribution of cash flows. They tended to dominate in the use of a varied rate of return to reflect currency risk while, consistent with this, relatively few of these firms made no currency risk adjustment. For all of these relationships, the phi measure of association was in the .200 to .250 range. In only one case could investment in Asia and the Far East be used as a predictor for the evaluation practice used.

Table 52

Relationship Between Investment in Asia and Use of Parent Cost of Debt for the Cost of Capital

	Use of Parent Cost of Debt as Cost of Capital		
Area of Investment	Not Used (Percent[a])	Used (Percent)	Total (Percent)
Asia and Far East	15.0	60.0	17.1
Not Asia and Far East	85.0	40.0	82.9
Total	95.2	4.8	100.0
Chi-Square = 6.79	1 Degree of Freedom		Significance = .009

[a] $N = 105$.

Table 53

Relationship Between Investment in Asia and Use of Probability Distribution of Cash Flows to Measure Business Risk

	Use of Probability Distribution to Measure Business Risk		
Area of Investment	Not Used (Percent[a])	Used (Percent)	Total (Percent)
Asia and Far East	12.5	32.0	17.1
Not Asia and Far East	87.5	68.0	82.9
Total	76.2	23.8	100.0
Chi-Square = 5.10	1 Degree of Freedom		Significance = .024

[a] $N = 105$.

Table 54

Relationship Between Investment in Asia and Use of Varied Rate to Return to Adjust for Currency Risk

	Use of Varied Rate of Return to Adjust for Currency Risk		
Area of Investment	Not Used (Percent[a])	Used (Percent)	Total (Percent)
Asia and Far East	9.3	25.5	17.1
Not Asia and Far East	90.7	74.5	82.9
Total	51.4	48.6	100.0

[a]N = 105.

Table 55

Relationship Between Investment in Asia and Making No Adjustment for Currency Risk

	Use of No Adjustment for Currency Risk		
Area of Investment	Not Used (Percent[a])	Used (Percent)	Total (Percent)
Asia and Far East	22.2	6.1	17.1
Not Asia and Far East	77.8	93.9	82.9
Total	68.6	31.4	100.0
Chi-Square = 4.16	1 Degree of Freedom		Significance = .041

[a]N = 105.

The results for the Asia and Far East group are difficult to interpret because the group includes developed countries like Japan as well as many LDCs. Given the findings of the present study, future research should pursue these relationships while carefully delineating the two subgroups.

The last group of significant relationships resulted for companies investing in Europe. There were five significant relationships. First, investment in Europe was significantly related to one measure of income from foreign investments, earnings after foreign taxes available for repatriation. As Table 56 indicates, firms investing in Europe tended not to use this measure. Only 3 of the 13 firms using it invested in Europe. The chi-square for this relationship was 4.48 with .034 significance. The phi coefficient was .207, but lambda was 0.00.

Table 56

Relationship Between Investment in Europe and Use of Earnings Available for Repatriation as Measure of Income

Area of Most Recent Investment	Not Used (Percent[a])	Used (Percent)	Total (Percent)
Europe	47.2	18.8	42.9
Not Europe	52.8	81.3	57.1
Total	84.8	15.2	100.0

[a] N = 105.

Investment in Europe was not related to any measure of investment for a foreign opportunity. It was significantly related to the use of two measures of business risk, calculating a probability of loss and use of "other" methods. The most common "other" method was simulation. The use of these sophisticated methods probably reflects the availability of information and the confidence of decision-makers in using this information in probability estimates. Firms investing in Europe dominate in the use of both measures. Tables 57 and 58 show the relationship between investment in Europe and use of probability of loss and "other" measures of business risk, respectively. The chi-square for the

Table 57

Relationship Between Investment in Europe and Use of

Probability of Loss to Measure Business Risk

Area of Investment	Use of Probability of Loss to Measure Business Risk		
	Not Used (Percent[a])	Used (Percent)	Total (Percent)
Europe	40.2	75.0	42.9
Not Europe	59.8	25.0	57.1
Total	92.4	7.6	100.0

Chi-Square = 4.12   1 Degree of Freedom   Significance = .042

[a]N = 105.

Table 58

Relationship Between Investment in Europe and Use of "Other"

Measures of Business Risk

Area of Investment	Use of "Other" Measures of Business Risk		
	Not Used (Percent[a])	Used (Percent)	Total (Percent)
Europe	41.2	100.0	42.9
Not Europe	58.8	0.0	57.1
Total	97.1	2.9	100.0

[a]N = 105.

relationship with probability of loss was 4.11 with .042 significance, while that for "other" measures of business risk was 4.12 with significance of .042. The phi coefficients were .198 for both measures, and neither had a positive lambda.

Investment in Europe was not related to any definitions of political risk, but it was related to use of sensitivity analysis and probability of loss as measures of political risk. Firms investing in Europe tended not to use sensitivity analysis but tended to dominate in the use of probability of loss as measures of political risk. Again, information availability seems to play a key role in the adoption of sophisticated methods. The cross-tabulation tables for these two variables are presented in Tables 59 and 60, respectively. The chi-square for both variables was 3.65 with .054 significance. Phi was .175 and .186, respectively. Neither variable had a positive lambda.

Investment in Europe did not show a significant relationship to any adjustments for political risk. Nor was it related to any definition, measure, or adjustment for currency risk.

To summarize, investment in Europe proved to have five significant relationships with investment evaluation practices. Firms investing in Europe were not as concerned with funds available for repatriation as other firms; i.e., they tended to take more of a local perspective in investment evaluation. This is consistent with the findings of the field study that several firms looked at their European companies as independent operations.

Firms investing in Europe dominated in the use of more sophisticated measures of business risk. This finding is consistent with results of the field study which indicated that firms rely on more sophisticated measures when information is available and reliable as it would tend to be in Europe. The same holds true for the lack of use of sensitivity analysis and the reliance on probability of loss to measure political risk by companies investing in Europe.

Relationships: Organizational Variables to Evaluation Practices

The results presented here describe the relationships discovered between organizational variables and foreign investment evaluation practices. Specific attention is given to the applicability of the results for the behavioral approach to corporate decision-making. The behavioral variables included objective of investment, organizational structure of foreign operations, decision-maker for foreign investments, specific purpose of investment, losses due to foreign risks, and rating of foreign risks for most recent FDMI. The investment evaluation practices were the same ones analyzed in the prior section, e.g., measures of income investment, cost of capital, business risk, etc. Again, 93 cross-tabulations were run for each independent organizational variable.

The organizational theory of firm behavior stresses the importance of

Table 59

Relationship Between Investment in Europe and Use of

Sensitivity Analysis to Measure Political Risk

	Use of Sensitivity Analysis to Measure Political Risk		
Area of Investment	Not Used (Percent[a])	Used (Percent)	Total (Percent)
Europe	47.1	25.0	42.9
Not Europe	52.9	75.0	57.1
Total	81.0	19.0	100.0
Chi-Square = 3.65	1 Degree of Freedom		Significance = .054

[a]N = 105.

Table 60

Relationship Between Investment in Europe and Use of

Probability of Loss to Measure Political Risk

	Use of Probability of Loss to Measure Political Risk		
Area of Investment	Not Used (Percent[a])	Used (Percent)	Total (Percent)
Europe	40.2	75.0	42.9
Not Europe	59.8	25.0	57.1
Total	92.4	7.6	100.0
Chi-Square = 3.65	1 Degree of Freedom		Significance = .054

[a]N = 105.

organizational structure to the way that corporate decisions are made and to the outcome of decisions. For example, Aharoni (1966) found that companies organized with an international division had a predisposition to undertake foreign investments; accordingly, at the outset of the study it was felt that the way a company was organized for foreign operations would impact the investment evaluation practices used to analyze foreign investments.

Five groups were created based on the companies' organizational structure today: organized globally by geographic area, by function, by product lines, in an international division or in a matrix. Cross-tabulations were then run between those groups and the 93 investment evaluation variables.[5] Only two statistically significant relationships were uncovered. Since that number could be due to spurious relationships, organizational structure was not found to be a good explanatory variable for foreign evaluation practices.

The behavioral theory also places importance on the impact of the decision-maker on corporate decision-making. The decision-maker is seen as influencing what factors are included in the analysis of a problem, i.e., how risks in a foreign investment decision are measured and what adjustments are made.

To test the relationship between decision-maker and foreign investment evaluation practices four separate sets of cross-tabulations were run: companies where the Board of Directors (BOD) was the decision-maker versus not; the companies where the Chief Executive Officer (CEO) was the decision-maker versus not; companies where the Chief Financial Officer (CFO) was the decision-maker versus not; and companies where the Area Manager was the decision-maker versus not. No significant relationships were found between the BOD as decision-maker and investment evaluation practices used, nor for CEO as decision-maker. Only two significant relationships were found for CFO as decision-maker and one for area manager. Thus, the decision-maker was not found to explain the investment evaluation practices used.

These results are somwhat at odds with the findings from the field study, in part reflecting the inability of a questionnaire to pick up the finer relationships in the decision process. In the majority of companies interviewed, the organizational structure impacted who initiated the foreign investment and what factors were included in the analysis of foreign investments. The decision-maker determined what criteria were used to evaluate an opportunity and what risk adjustments were made. These findings are discussed in more detail in the Field Study section.

The behavioral theory postulates that how a problem is defined impacts what factors are analyzed in searching for a solution. In the present context the problem is defined in terms of the specific reason for undertaking a foreign investment. Thus, four separate sets of cross-tabulations were run between the most common reasons for investing overseas and the evaluation practices used. The four groups included: invested to gain economies of scale versus all other reasons; invested to overcome tariff barriers versus all other reasons; invested to obtain government incentives versus all other reasons; invested because of government pressures to produce locally versus all other reasons. Of the 327 cross-tabulations, only 15 were significant. Since these could be due to spurious relationships, the reason for investment was not found to be a good explanatory variable of foreign evaluation practices.

Another basic postulate of the behavioral theory is that companies do not behave as if they seek to maximize profits only. Rather, they act to "satisfice" a number of objectives. The responses to question 1 in the first section of the questionnaire lend support to this. Although 80.0 percent of the companies responded that increasing profits was an objective of foreign investments, many companies stated they pursued multiple objectives in pursuing foreign opportunities.

In his application of the behavioral approach to the analysis of investment decisions in a computer company, Carter (1969) found that the more uncertain an opportunity the more criteria it was subjected to. To test for such a relationship in the present study, the investment evaluation practices of firms investing in their own industry overseas were compared to those for companies investing in another industry overseas. No significant relationships were discovered. As a further analysis, the number of practices each group used to define measure and adjust for business, political, and currency risk were compared. Again, no significant relationships were found. These findings may have resulted because although companies were investing overseas in an industry outside the primary industry of the parent, the parent did have domestic operations in that industry prior to the overseas investment. Thus, it was not viewed as riskier than an investment in the primary parent industry.

Three sets of variables consistent with the behavioral theory did prove to be statistically related to evaluation practices. One set of variables was the ranking that companies gave to the foreign risks for their most recent FDMI. Three groups were created of the companies, rating business risk, political risk, and currency risk most important. The importance a company placed on the various risks was significantly related to seven evaluation practices.

Rating of risk was not related to rating of the importance of financial criteria for evaluating investments. Nor was it related to the measure of income used in investment evaluation. There was a significant relationship between risk rating and use of purchase price to measure amount of investment.

As Table 61 shows, companies rating business risk most important dominated in the use of this measure, representing 68.8 percent of the companies using purchase price. The chi-square was 5.71 with a significance

Table 61

Relationship of Risk Rating to Use of Purchase Price
to Measure Investment

Type of Risk Most Important	Use of Purchase Price to Measure Investment		
	Not Used (Percent[a])	Used (Percent)	Total (Percent)
Business Risk	43.8	68.8	51.4
Currency Risk	28.8	18.8	25.7
Political Risk	27.4	12.5	22.9
Total	69.5	30.5	100.0

[a] N = 105.

Table 62

Relationship Between Risk Rating and Use of Local Cost of Equity
for Cost of Capital

Type of Risk Most Important	Use of Local Cost of Equity for Cost of Capital		
	Not Used (Percent[a])	Used (Percent)	Total (Percent)
Business Risk	52.5	33.3	51.4
Currency Risk	23.2	66.7	25.7
Political Risk	24.2	0.0	22.9
Total	92.3	5.7	100.0
Chi-Square = 6.01	2 Degrees of Freedom		Significance = .050

[a] N = 105.

of .05. The Cramer's V was .233, indicating a fair amount of association, but lambda was 0.00. The result is supported by evidence from the field study that when business (competitive) risk is high companies often enter the market via acquisition and so would tend to use purchase price as the investment measure.

Table 62 shows that risk rating was significantly related to use of local cost of equity for the cost of capital. Companies rating currency risk most important dominate in the use of this measure. The chi-square was 6.01 with .050 significance. Cramer's V was .239, but lambda was 0.00.

Risk rating showed no relationship to the measure of business risk. However, it was related to the use of varying the required payback as an adjustment for business risk. Table 63 shows that over half of the companies using this adjustment ranked business risk most important for their most recent FDMI. The chi-square was 7.00 with .030 significance. Cramer's V is .258, but again lambda was 0.00, indicating no predictive ability. This finding is consistent with the results of the field study which indicated that requiring a fast payback is a popular method to compensate for risks.

Paralleling this result, risk rating was significantly related to the practice of making no adjustment for business risk. Companies rating political risk most important made a disproportionate use of this practice. This result probably reflects the fact that companies tend to lump all risks together in the adjustment procedure, and where political risk is high it is typically analyzed qualitatively. Table 64 depicts the cross-tabulations between these variables. The chi-square was 6.69 with .035 significance. Although Cramer's V was .252, no predictive association was apparent.

Risk rating was not related to definitions or measures of political risk. As Table 65 shows, it was related to the adjustment for political risk, varying the required rate of return. Companies rating currency risk most important made disproportionate use of this adjustment. Chi-square was 7.11 with .029 significance. Cramer's V measure of association was .260 and a lambda of .125 indicates some predictive association.

Risk rating was significantly related to the use of the accounting definition of currency risk, FASB #8 exposure plus transactions in foreign currency. Table 66 shows that all of the companies using this definition of currency risk had rated currency risk most important. The chi-square was 5.89 with .050 significance. This finding is consistent with the field study result which indicated that when currency risk is important companies stress accounting definitions of exposure.

Risk rating was also significantly related to the use of the relatively sophisticated method of calculating a probability distribution of cash flows to measure currency risk. Table 67 shows that, as expected, the majority of firms using this measure were companies which rated currency risk important. The chi-square was 5.68 with .050 significance.

Table 63

Relationship Between Risk Rating and Use of Payback to Adjust for Business Risk

Type of Risk Most Important	Use of Payback to Adjust for Business Risk		
	Not Used (Percent[a])	Used (Percent)	Total (Percent)
Business Risk	49.3	56.7	51.4
Currency Risk	21.3	36.7	25.7
Political Risk	29.3	6.7	22.9
Total	71.4	28.6	100.0

Chi-Square = 7.00   2 Degrees of Freedom   Significance = .030

[a] N = 105.

Table 64

Relationship Between Risk Rating and Use of No Business Risk Adjustment

Type of Risk Most Important	Use of No Adjustment for Business Risk		
	Not Used (Percent[a])	Used (Percent)	Total (Percent)
Business Risk	52.5	48.0	51.4
Currency Risk	30.0	12.0	25.7
Political Risk	17.5	40.0	22.9
Total	76.2	23.8	100.0

Chi-Square = 6.69   2 Degrees of Freedom   Significance = .035

[a] N = 105.

Table 65

Relationship Between Risk Rating and Use of Varied Rate of Return to Adjust for Political Risk

	Use of Varied Rate of Return for Political Risk		
Type of Risk Most Important	Not Used (Percent[a])	Used (Percent)	Total (Percent)
Business Risk	54.2	49.1	51.4
Currency Risk	14.6	35.1	25.7
Political Risk	31.3	15.8	22.9
Total	45.7	54.3	100.0

Chi-Square = 7.11   2 Degrees of Freedom   Significance = .029

[a] N = 105.

Table 66

Relationship Between Risk Rating and Use of Accounting Exposure to Define Currency Risk

	Use of Accounting Exposure for Currency Risk		
Type of Risk Most Important	Not Used (Percent[a])	Used (Percent)	Total (Percent)
Business Risk	52.4	0.0	51.4
Currency Risk	24.3	100.0	25.7
Political Risk	23.3	0.0	22.9
Total	98.1	1.9	100.0

Chi-Square = 5.89   2 Degrees of Freedom   Significance = .050

[a] N = 105.

Table 67

Relationship Between Risk Rating and Use of Probability Distribution to Measure Currency Risk

	Use of Probability Distribution to Measure Currency Risk		
Type of Risk Most Important	Not Used (Percent[a])	Used (Percent)	Total (Percent)
Business Risk	52.7	42.9	51.4
Currency Risk	22.0	50.0	25.7
Political Risk	25.3	7.1	22.9
Total	86.7	13.3	100.0

Chi-Square = 5.68   2 Degrees of Freedom   Significance = .050

[a] N = 105.

Table 68

Relationship Between Risk Rating and Use of No Adjustment for Currency Risk

	Use of No Currency Risk Adjustment		
Type of Risk Most Important	Not Used (Percent[a])	Used (Percent)	Total (Percent)
Business Risk	52.8	48.5	51.4
Currency Risk	30.6	15.2	25.7
Political Risk	16.7	36.4	22.9
Total	68.6	31.4	100.0

Chi-Square = 6.01   2 Degrees of Freedom   Significance = .049

[a] N = 105.

Similarly, risk rating showed a significant relationship with the use of the practice of not adjusting for currency risk. Table 68 shows that a small percentage of firms using no adjustment rank currency risk most important. The chi-square is 6.01 with significance of .050.

Risk rating proved to have significant relationships with several of the evaluation practices used by MNCs. However, the relationships were not clearly consistent with those anticipated at the outset of the study. Initially, it was expected that companies ranking business risk most important would use sophisticated methods to measure and adjust for business risk. The same pattern was expected for companies rating political or currency risks most important. Only for companies rating currency risk most important were these expectations clearly borne out.

These results may reflect several factors. First, due to FASB #8 top management in many companies has placed particular emphasis on foreign currency losses and so investments in areas felt to exhibit high currency risk are scrutinized with the most sophisticated methods. Political and business risks may not have received this emphasis even for investments in areas where these are important risks. Second, information about currency movements may be more easily obtained than that about political risks which tend to be difficult to measure and quantify. Thus, managers would be more willing to apply the sophisticated techniques in high currency risk areas but prefer to leave information in qualitative form where political and business risks are high. This finding would be consistent with the importance of personal risk in explaining the risk analysis methods employed. This concept is discussed in detail in the Field Study section of the chapter.

The last set of significant relationships derived from the behavioral theory involves the loss history of companies. One of the key relational concepts of the behavioral theory is that organizations learn, that learning is strongly influenced by past experience, and that learning affects policies. In the present context it was postulated that the past loss record of a company due to foreign risks would impact the investment evaluation practices they would select. Specifically, companies with a history of foreign currency-related losses would develop and use more sophisticated currency risk definitions, measures, and adjustments. A parallel result was anticipated for companies suffering politically related losses.

To analyze these expected relationships, two groups were formed: one group had experienced negative effects from currency risks in the past 10 years and the other group had not. Cross-tabulations were run between currency loss record and the investment evaluation methods. Although six significant relationships were found, none of them related to currency risk definition, measurement, or adjustment.

Losses due to currency risks did have a significant relationship to the use of the dollar as the currency of analysis for foreign investments. This adoption of a parent company perspective was expected for companies experiencing losses. Table 69 shows that of the companies using dollars, 97.6 percent of them had suffered currency losses. The chi-square was 7.89 with .019 significance.

A similar analysis was undertaken for companies suffering a politically related loss overseas in the past 10 years. Political loss record was significantly related to 10 evaluation practices, but only two of them were with political evaluation practices.

As indicated in Table 70, political risk losses were significantly related to the use of operational restrictions to define political risk. Companies that had not suffered politically related losses tended not to use this definition. The chi-square was 3.79 with significance of .050. Since operational restrictions represent a more sophisticated definition of political risk, these results are as expected.

Similarly, companies which had politically related losses dominated in the use of the sophisticated measure of political risk, calculation of a probability of loss. Table 71 shows this relationship. Of the companies using this measure, 72.7 percent had political losses. The chi-square was 3.61 with .050 significance. Since probability of loss is one of the more sophisticated measures of political risk, the result is as anticipated. However, the record of political losses was not related to any adjustments for political risk.

These relationships lend some support to the learning concepts of the behavioral theory. More support comes from the field study results and will be dealt with in some detail in that section of this chapter.

Summary of Relationships: Demographic and Organizational Variables to Evaluation Practices

Two of the goals of this research were: one, to search for general relationships between firm characteristics and investment evaluation practices used, and two, to test relationships drawn from the behavioral theory of corporate decision-making. Several significant relationships were found between demographic variables and evaluation practices. Tests of relationships between organizational factors and evaluation practices resulted in mixed success.

Of the demographic factors, size of the firm (as measured by total foreign sales), geographic dispersion of the firm (as measured by the number of different areas worldwide where the firm had invested), and age of the firm as a multinational all showed significant relationships with several evaluation practices. However, the pattern of relationships for the age variable was not as

Table 69

Relationship Between Currency Losses and Currency of Evaluation for Foreign Investment

	Currency of Evaluation			
Loss Record	Dollars (Percent[a])	Local Currency (Percent)	Both (Percent)	Total (Percent)
Currency Loss	97.6	100.0	79.7	87.6
No Currency Loss	2.4	0.0	20.3	12.4
Total	39.0	4.8	56.2	100.0

Chi-Square = 7.89   2 Degrees of Freedom   Significance = .019

[a]N = 105.

Table 70

Relationship Between Political Losses and Use of Operational
Restrictions to Define Political Risk

	Use of Operational Restrictions to Define Political Risk		
Loss Record	Not Used (Percent[a])	Used (Percent)	Total (Percent)
Political Loss	29.6	51.3	45.7
No Political Loss	70.4	48.7	54.3
Total	25.7	74.3	100.0

Chi-Square = 3.79   1 Degree of Freedom   Significance = .050˙

[a]N = 105.

Table 71

Relationship Between Political Losses and Use of Probability of
Loss to Measure Political Risk

	Use of Probability of Loss to Measure Political Risk		
Loss Record	Not Used (Percent[a])	Used (Percent)	Total (Percent)
Political Loss	42.6	72.7	45.7
No Political Loss	57.4	27.3	54.3
Total	89.5	10.5	100.0

Chi-Square = 3.61   1 Degree of Freedom   Significance = .050

[a]N = 105.

had been expected. Possible reasons for this difference between the anticipated and actual results were discussed earlier. None of these demographic variables showed a strong relationship to the evaluation practices in a predictive sense.

Four other demographic variables that were tested for relationship to the evaluation practices did not prove significant. These variables included industry of investment, size of investment, method of investment, and ownership percentage for the firms' most recent FDMIs.

The demographic variables showing the most significant relationships with evaluation practices were the geographic areas of investment for the firms' most recent FDMIs. Investments in Europe, Latin America, and Asia and the Far East proved significant with a number of evaluation practices. Companies investing in Europe tended to take a local perspective more than companies investing in Latin America. Also, companies investing in Europe seemed to use more sophisticated risk evaluation practices. This result is consistent with a priori expectations and with the results of other recent studies.

In the tests of relationships grounded in the behavioral theory of firm decision-making, only two proved significant. Based on the behavioral theory, the organizational structure of the firm; the decision-maker for foreign opportunities; the reason for investment; and the industry of investment were expected to be related to the evaluation practices companies used. Based on the questionnaire results no such relationships were found. But the field study results indicate that the lack of relationships may reflect the limitations of the methodology to discern finer relationships.

Support was found for the assumption of the behavioral theory that firms seek to satisfy multiple goals, not just to maximize profits. Most of the firms in the study had both profit and growth goals when undertaking foreign investments.

It was felt that the relative importance of the various foreign risks for the companies' most recent FDMI would impact the risk evaluation practices used. Risk rating was found to be significantly related to eight evaluation practices.

Finally, one of the key relational concepts of the behavioral theory is that firms learn. In the present context it was felt that firms experiencing losses related to foreign risks would have developed and used more sophisticated risk evaluation methods than firms which had not. Six significant relationships were found between currency loss record and evaluation practices used. However, none of them related to currency risk definition, measurement, or adjustment. This may reflect learning by firms from the experience of others as well as directly. The recently well-publicized currency losses of many companies may have resulted in the adoption of common risk evaluation practices by most firms.

The findings for politically related losses were more in line with expectations. Political loss record was significantly related to 10 evaluation practices. Companies which had negative affects due to political changes overseas dominated in the use of sophisticated political risk definitions and measurements.

Thus, some support for relationships drawn from the behavioral theory was found in the statistical analysis of the questionnaire responses. More broad-based support comes from the answers to the telephone and personal interviews. A description of these responses follows next.

The Field Study

The analysis presented in this section is based on 15 telephone interviews and 10 personal visits with selected respondents to the mail questionnaire. Participants in the field study were chosen based on their answers to questions 5 and 8 in Section I, questions 2, 3, 7, and 11 in Section II, question 5 in Section III, and question 1 in Section IV of the questionnaire. (See Appendix B for a copy of the questionnaire.) The firms were selected in order to allow the researcher to explore a variety of responses to each question. As such, no special attempts were made to assure that the subsample reflected the distribution of responses in the overall sample.

However, as the following tables indicate, the subsample fairly closely paralleled the overall sample responses to the key questions. Table 72 compares the industry distribution of the 25-company group to the total sample. Of the main industry groups, only the paper industry was not represented in the subsample. The food products and chemical industries were represented more heavily on the subsample than in the 105-company total group.

Table 73 compares the area of most recent investment for the field group and the total sample. The field group invested less in Europe and more in all other areas of the world than the total sample. This may be due in part to the fact that many companies view investment in Europe as very much equal in terms of risk to investments in the United States. Thus, to obtain the diversity of evaluation practices desired in the field study, a higher percent of companies investing elsewhere was required.

Table 74 presents a comparison of the percentage of companies in each sample group that rated various financial criteria very important in evaluating foreign investments. This was the first of the key selection variables (question 5, Section I of the questionnaire). The field study group fairly closely paralleled the total sample except for a slight emphasis on companies favoring Internal Rate of Return in the field sample.

Table 72

Comparison of Parent Company Industry for Total Sample Versus Field Study Subsample

Total Sample (Percent[a])	Field Sample (Percent[b])	Industry
11.4	20.0	Food Products
4.8	2.0	Paper and Allied Products
24.8	32.0	Chemicals and Allied Products
2.9	4.0	Rubber Products
10.5	8.0	Primary and Fabricated Metals
17.1	22.0	Machinery (except electrical)
7.6	4.0	Electrical Machinery
8.6	8.0	Transportation Equipment
12.4	0.0	Other

[a] $N = 105$.

[b] $N = 25$.

Table 73

Comparison of Geographic Area of Most Recent Investment for Total Sample and Field Study Subsample

Total Sample (Percent[a])	Field Sample (Percent[b])	Geographic Area
42.9	16.0	Europe
1.9	4.0	Middle East
1.9	4.0	Africa
17.1	28.0	Asia and Far East
32.4	40.0	Latin America
1.9	8.0	Canada
1.9	0.0	Other

[a] N = 105.

[b] N = 25.

Table 75 shows a comparison between the two samples on the second key selection question, the cost of capital used in evaluating foreign investments (question 8, Section I of the questionnaire). Again, the field group fairly closely paralleled the total sample.

The ways that firms measure and adjust for business risk constituted other key selection questions (questions 2 and 3 in Section II of the questionnaire). These methods were used as a proxy for firms' practices regarding political risk and foreign currency risk as well, because most companies tended to use similar practices for all three risks. As Table 76 shows, the field study group was concentrated in those companies making a subjective evaluation or using a sensitivity analysis to measure business risk. These were the most common measures used in the total sample, and it was important to gain a complete understanding of their use.

Table 77 indicates that the field sample was slightly more concentrated in companies varying the required rate of return as an adjustment for business risk than the total sample. This was done in order to explore this answer in depth. However, all reported adjustment methods were represented in the field sample.

Table 74

Comparison of Ratings of Financial Criteria for Foreign Investments Between Total Sample and Field Study Subsample

For Most Recent FDMI		For FDMI Today		
Total Sample (Percent)[a]	Field Sample (Percent)	Total Sample (Percent)	Field Sample (Percent)	Financial Criteria
21.9	20.0	21.9	24.0	Payback
31.4	32.0	31.4	32.0	Accounting Return on Investment
6.7	4.0	8.6	8.0	Return on Sales
41.9	56.0	46.7	56.0	Internal Rate of Return
15.2	12.0	13.3	12.0	Net Present Value
15.2	12.0	18.1	8.0	Contribution to Earnings per Share

[a]These figures represent the percent of the total sample of 105 firms and the field sample of 25 firms which rated each financial criterion as very important.

Table 75

Comparison of Cost of Capital Used by Total Sample and Field Study Subsample to Evaluate Foreign Investments

| For Most Recent FDMI || For FDMI Today || Definition of Cost of Capital |
Total Sample (Percent[a])	Field Sample (Percent[b])	Total Sample (Percent[a])	Field Sample (Percent[b])	
				Parent
4.8	8.0	5.7	8.0	Cost of Debt
7.6	12.0	7.6	8.0	Cost of Equity
50.5	56.0	50.5	60.0	Weighted Average
				Local
7.6	8.0	7.6	8.0	Cost of Debt
5.7	12.0	5.7	1.2	Cost of Equity
21.9	24.0	22.9	28.0	Weighted Average
13.4	16.0	14.4	16.0	Other

NOTE: Percents do not total 100 because companies used more than one definition.

[a] N = 105.

[b] N = 25.

Table 76

Comparison of Measure of Business Risk Used by Companies in Total Sample Versus Companies in Field Study Subsample

For Most Recent FDMI		For FDMI Today		Measure of Business Risk
Total Sample (Percent[a])	Field Sample (Percent[b])	Total Sample (Percent[a])	Field Sample (Percent[b])	
86.8	84.0	83.8	84.0	Make a subjective evaluation of risk
23.8	36.0	25.7	36.0	Project a probability distribution of cash flows
3.8	4.0	5.7	4.0	Estimate the covariance of cash flows with other investment cash flows
46.7	84.0	47.6	84.0	Perform a sensitivity analysis
7.6	8.0	10.5	12.0	Calculate the probability of loss
2.9	1.0	1.9	1.0	Make no risk assessment
2.9	0.0	3.8	0.0	Other

NOTE: Percents do not total 100 because companies used more than one measure.

[a] N = 105.

[b] N = 25.

Table 77

Comparison of Adjustments Made in Capital-Budgeting Procedures to Reflect Business Risk for Total Sample Versus Field Study Subsample

For Most Recent FDMI		For FDMI Today		Adjustment to Reflect Business Risk
Total Sample (Percent[a])	Field Sample (Percent[b])	Total Sample (Percent[a])	Field Sample (Percent[b])	
57.1	68.0	60.0	72.0	Vary rate of return required from the FDMI
21.0	24.0	25.7	28.0	Vary cost of capital used in discounted cash flow analysis
28.6	32.0	28.6	36.0	Vary payback period required from the FDMI
1.9	1.0	2.9	1.0	Insure risks and charge cash flows for these costs
5.7	12.0	5.7	12.0	Charge cash flows for cost of insuring risks even if not taken
23.8	16.0	18.1	16.0	Make no adjustment for risk
7.6	12.0	8.6	8.0	Other

NOTE: Percents do not total 100 because companies used more than one adjustment.

[a] N = 105.
[b] N = 25.

For question 7 in Section II on the currency of investment evaluation, the field sample was fairly evenly split between those using dollars only and those using dollars and local currency both. Question 11 in Section II was used as a selection variable in order to insure that the field sample contained companies that had experienced either politically related or foreign currency losses overseas.

Question 5 in Section III was used to insure that some of the field study firms had a foreign investment under evaluation today in the hopes that an actual decision might be observed. This did not prove to be possible due to the long time span covered by the decision process.

Finally, question 1 in the final section of the questionnaire was used to attempt to incorporate as may companies whose practices changed over time in the field sample as possible. The results of these field interviews are presented in the rest of this section.

The results presented in the remainder of this section are based on 25 personal and telephone interviews. The questions asked in these interviews were designed to allow the researcher to gain insight into the organizational context of foreign investment decisions and also to better understand how foreign risks are evaluated. (A list of the questions pursued in the field interviews is presented in Appendix C.)

At the outset of each interview the respondent was asked to describe his role in this company's most recent FDMI decision. Typically, the respondent was not the original initiator of the investment proposal nor the final decision-maker. His involvement was after a project had reached the formal written proposal stage. Usually, he was responsible for reviewing the assumptions of a proposal, requesting additional information from the proposing group, and making a go-no go recommendation for the final decision-maker. In one case the respondent was the final decision-maker and in one he had not been with the company when the most recent FDMI decision was made.

Respondents were next asked to give an overview of the foreign investment decision process including such factors as who initially suggested that a foreign investment be undertaken, what organizational path a proposal took, and what was required in a project proposal at each stage. How a company was organized for global operations impacted each of these factors.

The field sample was fairly evenly split between firms organized in worldwide product lines, those organized geographically for international operations, and those using a combination of the two. Companies using international product groups tended to follow a top-down suggestion approach; i.e., worldwide product managers suggested foreign investment opportunities consistent with their global strategic, profit, and sales goals. These were often derived from the prior year's budgeting process. Local product managers were then responsible for developing the investment proposal.

Once this proposal had been developed, it typically was submitted to a corporate headquarters business development group and to the Chief Financial Officers (CFO) group (or Treasury function) for review. Finally, the proposal would reach the Chief Executive Officer (CEO) for final decision. If the project was above some set dollar amount (usually around $2 million), Board of Directors approval was also required.

Companies organized in geographic areas tended to favor a bottom-up suggestion approach; i.e., local managers suggested investments in their area to regional managers. In many cases these companies also had an international division. If so, the proposal flowed there and at the same time to the Treasury function for review. If the company had no international division, the proposal went from the regional manager to corporate planning staff and the Treasury function for review. The final steps in either case were to the CEO and possibly the Board for approval.

In companies organized with both product and geographic group worldwide, foreign investments suggestions flowed two ways, top-down in product groups and bottom-up in geographic groups. In these cases each group presented proposals to the other for review. The proposal then typically went to the CFO for review and recommendation to the CEO. Finally, the proposal had to receive the Board of Directors' approval.

The initiator of a project impacted the factors which were stressed in the investment proposal. Worldwide product managers were typically most concerned with the strategic fit of a proposed investment and with sales factors, e.g., market size, market share, potential growth, and competitors. The projects which they proposed stressed these factors while profit measures and financial evaluations received secondary consideration.

Projects proposed by local or regional managers stressed profit and budget factors. Financial factors such as return on investment, earnings contribution, etc. were emphasized in these project proposals.

In addition to the importance of the initiator on what factors were considered in an investment analysis, the level in the organization that a proposal reached impacts it as well. In the early stages of investment analysis, marketing factors and crude risk screens tended to prevail. By the time a project reached the formal proposal stage (at least by the time it reached either the corporate planning or international division at headquarters), financial factors were included. Many companies reported that financial criteria were key in the final decision by the CEO.

It should be noted that the final outcome of the decision process resulted from a good deal of negotiation between the groups involved in the process. For example, one respondent described the decision as follows: The project was proposed by a local subsidiary manager orally to his regional manager. The regional manager felt the project had merit and requested a general proposal. After reviewing this proposal the regional staff prepared a more detailed report augmenting the financial factors analyzed. This report was then returned to the local staff for review and changes. The proposal went from there to the CFO whose group challenged the exchange rate and financing assumptions. The report went back to regional staff for changes and justifications of assumptions. It then went to the CEO for a decision. The CEO had final responsibility for deciding what rate of return was appropriate for the project. He conferred with both the regional staff and the CFO in making this determination. This type of negotiation was typical for the majority of the field survey companies.

The importance of these organizational factors in the foreign investment decision process has implications for how corporate resources would be allocated in various firms. Aharoni (1966) found that the more powerful the initiating force the more likely a project was to be accepted. It seems then that because of their top-down approach companies organized in product lines would be more likely to accept foreign projects than those organized in geographic areas. Second, companies organized in product lines seem more likely to consider projects in areas outside their present operating locations overseas. However, with their emphasis on strategic and sales goals it would appear that companies organized in product lines would be less likely to achieve the efficient allocation of economic theory than geographically organized firms employing profit goals. Finally, the negotiation process typical of the investment decision underscores the satisficing behavior of investment decision making, the allocative impacts which have been discussed earlier in this chapter.

All of these findings are consistent with the behavioral theory of firm decision-making. However, in addition to organizational factors, factors peculiar to an investment itself also impacted the evaluation practices companies used.

For example, in most of the companies interviewed, formal project proposals followed a standard format whether the proposal was for a new typewriter or the acquisition of a plant overseas. Clearly, the substance of the proposal varied markedly, depending on the type of project. Beyond this, very basic and important differences in the financial criteria used, the scope of the evaluation, and the risk analysis undertaken depended on project characteristics. Since most of the companies invested overseas in projects similar to ones they already operated, the key differentiating characteristic was geographic area of investment.

During the personal and telephone interview, respondents were asked how the importance of financial criteria for evaluating opportunities changed for domestic versus foreign investments and for foreign investments in various geographic areas. Almost all of the respondents indicated that the same financial criteria were used to evaluate all investments worldwide. The one exception was the importance of payback period. Over half of the respondents indicated that payback was a more important criterion for overseas investments than for domestic. It was used most often to evaluate investments in LDCs as a way of compensating for political risks. All but two of the companies said that potential investments in DCs were considered of equal risk to domestic investments and were subjected to identical criteria. The implications of these practices for corporate resource allocation were discussed earlier in this chapter.

By far the most important criterion used to evaluate foreign opportunities was a return on investment measure. Internal rate of return was used most often with accounting rate of return second. As mentioned before, payback was often used in conjunction with these measures. Contribution to earnings per share was rarely used, and when it was it was used in the analysis of acquisitions. Net present value was the least popular evaluation criterion.

These findings differ from those of a recent study by Bavishi (1979). They are also somewhat at odds with the findings of Schall et al. (1978) and Klammer (1972) on domestic evaluation criteria. These discrepancies are discussed more fully in Chapter 7.

When asked if they believed that foreign investments were inherently riskier than domestic investments, 75 percent of the companies responded yes. They cited foreign currency and political risks of foreign opportunities as the reasons. Only five companies said that it depended on the total risk profile and that sometimes lower business risk overseas could compensate for the other risk, making a foreign investment less risky than a domestic one. Significantly, since most companies lump all foreign risks together in their analyses, they cannot specify individual risks. This practice may result in misallocation of resources away from LDCs, in particular where low competitive risks might compensate for other risks.

Along these same lines the respondents were asked whether the cost of capital used in investment evaluation varied for domestic versus foreign investments, for investments in various areas overseas, or for different types of projects. The typical answer was that the cost of capital used for investments was loosely based on a weighted average parent cost. This cost was used as a basic hurdle rate that all investments, regardless of area or type of project, had to meet. This standard was then adjusted subjectively to reflect the risks of a project.

Seven companies did not follow this basic pattern. For these companies the cost of capital was still used as a hurdle rate that an investment had to meet. However, instead of having a standard basic rate worldwide, the cost of capital was derived from the cost of financing a project locally. This rate in turn could be subjectively adjusted to reflect the business, political, and currency risks of the project.

In most companies interviewed, business risk was measured and adjusted for using the more sophisticated methods with political and currency risks using the same or less sophisticated methods. Several reasons were given for this pattern. First, political risk was often used as an initial screen and would determine whether a project came to the formal proposal stage. Thus, it was not evaluated in detail in later analyses. Currency risk was most often dealt with through changes in operating policies rather than in the investment evaluation process. Finally, a majority of companies stated that they used more sophisticated measures for business risk because they had a greater amount of and more reliable information on this factor. Thus, a quantitative analysis was meaningful and justified.

For all three risks, by far the most common method of measurement was a subjective evaluation. But for business risk, the use of a sensitivity analysis was a close second. Twenty-one of the 25 firms interviewed included a sensitivity analysis in their project proposals usually conducted on best, worst, and most likely price and volume estimates. Only nine of these companies went so far as to attach probabilities to the price and volume estimates to obtain a probability distribution of cash flows. Three companies calculated the probability of loss, and one each made no risk assessment and estimated the covariance of cash flows with those of other projects.

The companies justified their preference for subjective evaluation by the lack of reliable information. They chose sensitivity analysis as opposed to the other measures because they felt it gave the final decision-maker the broadest view of the investment assumptions and possible outcomes. Ten companies said that the more quantitative measures gave a picture of precision that was unjustified. Seven companies said that the more sophisticated measures were not understood at top levels of management. In these cases use of management science techniques to measure risks was seen as increasing personal risk and so they were not adopted.

Consistent with their preference for return measures to evaluate foreign investments, the most common adjustment to reflect business risk was varying the rate of return required from a project. Sixteen of the companies made this adjustment. The next most popular method was to vary the required payback, used by eight companies. Seven firms varied the cost of capital and five made no adjustment.

The amount of adjustment tended to be highly subjective based on the "experience," "gut feel," and "enlightened intuition" of the decision-maker. This result is consistent with the findings presented earlier, and the allocative effects were presented there as well. Projects received little comparative analysis, so projects of similar risks may or may not have received equivalent adjustments. Measurement of business risk was accomplished by methods that did not lend themselves easily to translation into standard risk adjustments.

Only one company interviewed was attempting to standardize the amount of adjustment for countries of similar risk. A group of four senior executives classified countries into three groups. The required rate of return from a project depended on which group the country fell in. The executives classified countries judgmentally based on published country risks ratings, bank currency reports, and the opinions of local operating managers. Most companies felt that this type of procedure was still highly subjective, ignored project/country risk interactions, and resulted in artificial categorization of countries.

One broad categorization of countries made by most companies was between LDCs and DCs. Investments in LDCs were consistently required to earn a higher return (or quicker payback, etc.) than those in DCs. Little emphasis was placed on determining project-specific risks within these broad classifications, which may bias investment flows away from LDCs.

This same type of categorization characterized many companies' treatment of political risk. In defining political risk, 18 of the companies interviewed said that they considered the same factors worldwide. The most important factors were expropriation or nationalization, restrictions on repatriations, and operational restrictions. However, most companies stated that the importance of the various political factors shifted for investments in LDCs versus DCs. Companies tended to emphasize expropriation and breaches of contracts as the main sources of risk in LDCs and operational restrictions in DCs. Repatriation restrictions were important everywhere.

The measurement of political risk followed the methods used for business risk. Subjective evaluation was relied upon even more for political risk than business risk. Twenty-three of the 25 companies used this measurement practice. Second most important was sensitivity analysis, with 16 companies using it. The other measures received only limited usage.

Twenty companies said that political factors were presented in a qualitative manner, often only a descriptive section in a project proposal. This fact is reflected in the finding that four of the companies made no adjustment in their capital-budgeting procedures to reflect political risk. Of the companies making an adjustment, most varied the required rate of return. Nineteen of the 25 companies made this adjustment. Varied payback was used to adjust for political risk more often than for business risk, being used by 12 companies.

However, as was the case for business risk, the adjustments tended to be highly subjective. Although 17 of the companies subscribed to some outside service which ranked countries according to risk, only one company attempted to reflect these risk ratings in standard relative adjustments in financial performance required from an investment.

In addition, the majority of companies failed to adjust for each risk separately. They tended to lump all risks together and make a single adjustment, one which rarely took the time pattern of risks into account. For example, one firm expected expropriation in the sixth year of the project, so they raised the discount rate used in their discounted cash flow analysis. In effect, this adjustment arbitrarily penalized the earlier cash flows.

The pattern of using qualitative measures to analyze risks followed through to foreign currency risk as well. Twenty-one of the companies interviewed made a subjective evaluation of currency risk. This evaluation was usually made in the Treasury function, although nine of the companies had a separate foreign exchange department to make this evaluation. Companies relied heavily on outside sources, primarily banks, in gathering information to project future currency rates.

The majority of companies used a single point estimate of the future exchange rate projected from three to five years in evaluating a foreign project. Five companies simply used the current exchange rate in foreign investment evaluations. Eight companies performed a sensitivity analysis to measure currency risk based on three estimates of the future rate. The final evaluation was always done in dollars, using the most likely estimate.

The reasons companies gave for using fairly qualitative currency risk measures were similar to the ones given for business and political risk, lack of reliable information which led to a feeling of personal risk. Consistent with this is the use of subjective adjustments in capital-budgeting procedures to reflect currency risk. Nine of the companies made no adjustment for currency risk. They felt that currency risks were better adjusted for through changes in operating policies than in adjustments to criteria for evaluating investments.

The area of greatest diversity among the companies interviewed was in the definition of exposure to currency changes. The field respondents were fairly evenly split between those companies emphasizing accounting definitions of exposure versus those using a cash flow approach. The 10 companies using an accounting approach as their primary definition stated that FASB #8 had focused management attention on the earnings impact of currency shifts. Thus, they were an important element in investment evaluation.

Twelve companies used a cash flow definition of currency exposure. They believed that FASB #8 might impact their financing decisions but should not enter into the investment evaluation process. However, eight of these companies said that the accounting impact of an investment was usually presented as a supplemental analysis.

All of the companies interviewed in the field study had experienced negative effects in the past 10 years due to political or currency factors. They were asked what impact these losses had had in the way that subsequent investment opportunities in the same geographic area were analyzed. The majority of companies, 17 of 25, responded that the losses did not result in specific changes in the way that business, political, or currency risks were defined, measured, or adjusted for. The basic procedures remained the same, but the amount and importance of the analysis increased.

As stated before, currency transaction losses had focused management attention on currency risks. Thus, many companies stated that in areas where they had suffered currency losses an analysis of the options available to reduce exposure for an investment became a standard part of project proposals. Similarly, in areas where companies had suffered political losses, a descriptive analysis of the current political environment became a standard part of a project proposal. Overall, losses appeared to make companies more aware of risks, to emphasize them qualitatively in investment analysis, but not to change investment evaluation practices.

Finally, the companies were asked if they felt that environmental differences ought to be reflected in the analyses of investments. All agreed that they should. But when asked if their practices accomplished this, 21 said no. The primary areas of deficiency were: (1) forecasting of future events, (2) quantifying risks, and (3) reflecting risks consistently in the evaluation system. The primary obstacles to improved decision-making mentioned by the respondents were lack of management understanding of the sophisticated methods and increasing instability overseas. This instability reinforced the justifications given for using qualitative analyses.

The results of the telephone and personal interviews gave a composite picture of a foreign investment decision process characterized by: (1) noncomparative analysis with a parent-company focus, (2) a qualitative approach to risk analysis, and (3) a subjective approach to risk adjustment. The consistency of the results with those of similar research efforts follows in the next chapter.

7
Summary and Conclusions

This final chapter begins with a summary of the purpose, methodology, and background of the study. A comparison of the results of prior studies and the results of the present study follows this summary. These comparisons are with earlier research in the areas of international decision-making, domestic capital budgeting, and behavioral approaches to corporate decision-making. The actual results of the current study are next compared to the anticipated results. The chapter ends with a discussion of the future research for which this work should provide a base.

Summary of Study Purpose, Methodology, and Background

The impact of the MNC on the economic, social, and political well-being of the countries in which it operates has long been an area of considerable controversy. This controversy has generated a wealth of studies falling into four broad categories: positive theories of direct investment at the aggregate level; theoretical and empirical research into the impact of foreign investment on home and host country economies; normative theories of direct investment at the firm level; and positive analysis of the foreign investment decision at the firm level.

Unfortunately, empirical evaluations of the positive theories of direct investment at the aggregate level have not produced general agreement on the superiority of any one explanation. In the second category, the impact of MNCs on the home and host economy is still open to debate. Normative theories of foreign direct investment, the third category, parallels the first two areas in the lack of agreement between prominent theories. Application of traditional domestic capital-budgeting approaches to the more complex international environment has left unanswered such issues as: Whose cash flows, parent or subsidiary, should be used in investment evaluation? Whose cost of capital is relevant for discounted cash flow analysis? How should the additional risks in international business, e.g., foreign exchange and political risk, be incorporated? Several steps have been taken toward answering these questions, as well as some of the issues in the first two categories, by the positive analysis of the international investment decision at the firm level. One of the earliest and most comprehensive of these studies was by Aharoni, who analyzed the foreign investment decision from a behavioral theory approach.

As G.P.E. Clarkson states, "whether one desires to construct a positive theory or to compare the results of a normative theory with existing procedures, a knowledge of actual behavior is a prerequisite"(Clarkson, 1962, pp. 1-2). Such a prerequisite has only begun to be fulfilled by the research to date. This study sought to expand the understanding of the international investment decision process by focusing on actual behavior of multinational companies. Thus, the goals of the research were to:

1. Document the international investment motives and evaluation practices used by a sample of U.S.-based manufacturing MNCs.
2. Discover the significant variables and relationships between variables in the international investment decision process of MNCs.
3. Test broad hypotheses on international investment decision-making drawn from the behavioral theory framework.

The data for the study were collected by conducting a two-phase exploratory field study. The first phase required developing and mailing a questionnaire, and the second involved interviewing selected survey respondents.

The questionnaire was designed to include questions pertaining to the general foreign investment evaluation practices of the firms: the methods they used to analyze the business, political, and foreign currency risks of foreign investments, and demographic information for classification of the firms. The section on general evaluation practices included questions on the objectives and reasons for making foreign investments, the decision-maker for foreign investments, the definitions of income, investment, and cost of capital used for foreign investments, and the financial criteria used to evaluate foreign opportunities. The questions in the second section focused on the practices firms used to define and measure risks in foreign investments and also the adjustments firms made to reflect these risks in their capital-budgeting procedures. The section on demographic information sought data about the characteristics of the firm's most recent foreign direct manufacturing investment (e.g., size, location, industry, etc.) as well as information on the firm itself (e.g., size, foreign commitments, geographic spread, industry, etc.).

The questionnaire was mailed to 255 companies. Each firm was identified as a U.S.-based manufacturing company that ranked in the *Fortune 500* for 1977 and controlled subsidiaries in at least six countries abroad. One hundred and eight firms completed and returned the questionnaire. The response rate for eligible firms was 52 percent. Firms were labeled ineligible if they had gone out of business, merged with another firm, or did not control manufacturing subsidiaries in at least six countries in 1978. The overall response rate for the study was 60.8 percent.

The criteria for participation in the second phase of the field study was based on the analysis of key questions on the questionnaire. This analysis was an attempt to contact firms with different policies toward foreign investment evaluation in order to acquire an in-depth explanation as to why certain policies were followed and alternatives were not. The analysis of key questions also sought to insure that all of the most common evaluation practices were examined in the field interviews to enable the researcher to clearly understand their use in various firms.

Ten firms were visited personally by the researcher, and an additional 15 firms were contacted by telephone. The purpose of these interviews was to gain a more thorough understanding of particular responses, to highlight the organizational context of the decision process, to explore the reasoning behind established foreign investment evaluation practices, and to uncover the most important problems in foreign investment analysis.

Comparison of Prior and Present Studies

The results of the current study are compared with the findings of three groups of earlier research: prior studies of international investment evaluation practices of MNCs; recent research on domestic capital-budgeting practices of U.S. companies; and research using the behavioral approach to analyze firm decision-making.

Comparison: Earlier Research on International Investment Evaluation and Present Research

The investment decision behavior of the present sample of MNCs is characterized by:

1. noncomparative, go-no analysis.
2. acceptable-level decision making as opposed to maximization behavior.
3. multiple objectives as a guide to behavior.

These results are consistent with the findings of earlier positive research into international investment decision-making.

In the mid-1960s, Polk et al. researched the impact of foreign investments on the U.S. balance of payments using a survey of 100 U.S. companies. Two of

Polk's findings are supported by the present research. Polk found that companies sought market and growth in making foreign investments. Profits were only one of several objectives leading to investments abroad. In the present research 80 percent of the companies selected profits as an objective for foreign investments but nearly half stated growth was also a goal. Forty-three percent of the companies indicated market share was an important goal as well.

Polk found that most companies analyze investments independently from other opportunities available. "Most companies do not have a master plan for international investments arrived at through careful evaluation of the various possibilities of employing capital so as to maximize the return on it" (Polk, 1966, p. 73). The results of the present study are consistent with this finding. Seventy-one percent of the respondents indicated that each investment alternative is evaluated on its own merits and a go-no go decision is made.

Four other studies by Aharoni (1966), Stonehill and Nathanson (1968), Piper (1971), and Bavishi (1979) are consistent with this result. These results indicate a long-term and continuing divergence between actual behavior and the behavior expected from theory based on the traditional economic model of the firm. The actual decision behavior should result in an inefficient allocation of resources when compared to that resulting from prescribed practices. Specifically, when the above practices are combined with the investment evaluation methods and risk analysis techniques used by the MNCs, the allocation of resources seems to be biased toward those with quick returns and against those with low initial profitability but long-term potential, against risky projects even if risks occur far in the future, and against projects in less developed countries.

In terms of the financial criteria used to evaluate foreign opportunities, the present research found that internal rate of return, accounting return on investment, and payback were the most popular. These findings are fairly consistent with the recent research by Bavishi (1979) but show an increased sophistication in criteria from Polk's (1966) study. Polk found that the companies were fairly equally divided between those using a return on sales criterion and those using a return on investment criterion. He found that few of the companies using a sales criterion employed discounted cash flow analysis (DCF). Also, although these companies examined a payback period, the majority did not find it of major importance.

The results of the present study indicate that return on sales measures are no longer an important foreign investment criterion. Only 8.6 percent of the 105 companies in the current study rated return on sales as very important in foreign investment evaluation. Consistent with the prescriptions of normative theory, most companies used a discounted cash flow approach to generating a rate of return on which to evaluate foreign investments. Payback period was rated very important by 22 percent of the companies but was never the sole investment criterion.

When the firms were asked how their foreign investment evaluation practices had changed in the past 10 years, the most common response was that they now employed more sophisticated practices. They cited the use of DCF analysis as an important change. These changes are consistent with the differences found between Polk's findings and those of the current research. The adoption of the DCF analysis indicates an improvement in investment evaluation practices which should imply an improved allocation of resources. However, the reliance on payback criteria overseas, especially for projects in LDCs, biases resource allocation in favor of projects with high initial returns and so may cause firms to reject projects with long-term profitability.

In terms of the definitions of income and investment used today by MNCs to evaluate foreign projects, the present research found that most companies used a dual approach. These findings are consistent with those of Bavishi (1979) and an earlier study by Stonehill and Nathanson (1968).

The Stonehill and Nathanson study focused specifically on the capital-budgeting practices of MNCs. They surveyed 219 U.S. firms and 100 foreign firms and they conducted interviews with 14 of the survey respondents. They found that firms were split between those using an earnings approach versus those that use a cash flow approach for foreign income. Stonehill and Nathanson found that 29 percent used earnings, 48 percent cash flow, and 23 percent "other". In the present study the percentages were much closer, with 53 percent using earnings and 44 percent cash flow. Many companies used both approaches, a method originally advocated in the Stonehill and Nathanson research. The adoption of this dual approach reflects companies' awareness that the growing demand of many countries for local ownership means that increasingly subsidiary objectives may differ from those of the parent. Therefore, the project should be profitable from both perspectives to be accepted.

In terms of the cost of capital, the present study indicated that the majority of firms use a parent weighted average cost, but nearly 35 percent of the firms use a local cost. The results parallel those of Bavishi (1979), who found that 43 percent of the companies applied a global weighted average cost of capital and 27 percent the cost of local financing.

When Stonehill and Nathanson (1968) questioned firms on their definition of the cost of capital, they found that 22 firms did not use a cost of capital at all. Of the ones that did, 64 percent used a standard cost of capital worldwide. Only 10 companies used a local cost of capital to analyze foreign investments. In the present study, only eight of the 105 respondents did not use a cost of capital. These changes parallel the increase in sophistication, i.e., use of DCF analysis, of foreign investment practices cited by respondents in the present study.

In the analysis of risks for foreign investments, companies have shown far less adoption of sophisticated methods than in their general evaluation practices. First, the range of risk variables considered is fairly limited. This finding is consistent with the recent study by Bavishi and an earlier study by Piper (1971).

Piper reviewed the foreign evaluation practices of 22 companies that presented feasibility studies under the AID Foreign Investment Survey Program. He also interviewed selected executives. As opposed to the other two studies presented here, Piper did not use only survey methodology. Instead, he also studied the actual feasibility reports developed by the firms.

Piper found that six categories of variables were considered by firms evaluating foreign investments. Financial considerations were by far the most important. Political and social considerations as well as marketing considerations received only slight attention.

Marketing considerations were found to be important in the present study, with nearly a quarter of the firms giving them as the specific reason for making foreign investments. In addition, the results of the personal and telephone interviews indicated that depending on the initiator of an investment proposal, marketing factors sometimes received priority over financial factors. The finding of the present research that political factors often act as an initial investment screen may explain Piper's finding on the lack of consideration of these factors in feasibility studies.

Of the risk factors considered, the methods of measurement differ markedly from those advocated in normative theory. For example, firms rarely use probability estimates to measure business risk and even less for political and currency risks. Instead, risk evaluation tends to be highly subjective, based to a large extent on long-term personal impressions and broad categorizations of risk classes, e.g., LDC versus DC. Rarely are risks analyzed with a project-specific focus.

Due to the subjective, noncomparative approach most companies take in measuring foreign risk, their adjustments to reflect these risks tend to be highly subjective as well. The most common approach is to lump all risks into a single increase in required returns or a faster payback. But these adjustments are not standardized to reflect relative risks between projects.

These findings are consistent with those of Stonehill and Nathanson as well as the recent research by Bavishi. Stonehill and Nathanson inquired as to how firms allowed for varying degrees of risk in various countries. The most common response was a subjective evaluation, with varying the required return on investment second. Bavishi found that over half of his respondents varied the required returns to reflect risk. In the present research 60 percent of the firms made this adjustment to reflect business risk, 57 percent for political risk, and 50 percent for currency risk. Bavishi also found that MNCs placed more importance on risk factors in LDCs than in DCs. But for any overseas project, risk assessment tended to be judgmental and subjective.

Overall, the findings on the risk analysis practices of MNCs indicate a persistent divergence from the methods prescribed in normative theory. These divergences imply a suboptimal allocation of corporate resources. First, the subjective, noncomparative, non-project-specific evaluation of risks appears to result in a bias against projects in LDCs. The practice of lumping all risks into a single adjustment results in a bias against projects with one especially risky factor. Also, the practice of raising the required return ignores the time pattern of risks and penalizes all project cash flows, thus resulting in a bias against projects with risks far in the future.

Comparison: Earlier Research on Domestic Capital-Budgeting Practices and Present Study

As part of the present research, firms were asked to describe the differences between their domestic and foreign investment evaluation practices. The majority responded that there were no important differences except for the consideration of political and foreign currency risks for foreign projects. The actual evaluation practices and procedures used remain the same.

The results of two recent studies in domestic capital-budgeting procedures seem to support this finding. In a 1972 study, Klammer surveyed 184 firms about their capital-budgeting practices. He found that 45 percent of the respondents used some formal risk adjustment technique, with raising the required return for a risky project the most common method. The same result held true for the present research.

Klammer also found that DCF methods were used by the majority of companies. The favorite evaluation criteria were, in order: internal rate of return, accounting rate of return, and payback. These results parallel those of the present study.

In a later study, Schall et al. (1978) found that domestic capital-budgeting practices had become more sophisticated since Klammer's 1970 research. Their findings are based on the responses of 189 firms to a mail survey. They found that companies used payback most often as a financial criterion, followed by internal rate of return, accounting rate of return, and net present value, in that order. Again, payback was not as an important criterion in the present study, being secondary to internal rate of return. Most of the companies in Schall's research used internal rate of return with payback, which is consistent with the present findings for international capital budgeting.

Schall found that nearly half of the firms use a weighted average cost of capital as a discount rate. Similarly, in the present research the majority of companies use a standard cost of capital worldwide based on the parent weighted average.

Schall et al. confirmed Klammer's findings that firms attempted to adjust for risk in capital-budgeting procedures by adjusting the required return, shortening the payback, or raising the discount rate. The results of the present study indicate that companies make similar adjustments for overseas risks.

Comparison: Research Using the Behavioral Approach and Results of Present Study

The analytical framework of the behavioral theory as proposed by Cyert and March (1962) consisted of three main variables (organizational goals, expectations, and choice) and four relational concepts (quasi-resolution of conflict, uncertainty avoidance, problematic search, and organizational learning). These elements of the behavioral theory were described in an earlier chapter. Results of the present study expected from the behavioral approach are compared to the actual results in the next section of this chapter. However, first it is useful to compare the results of the current research with those of two earlier studies which applied the behavioral framework to analyzing corporate decisions.

In a 1969 study, Carter examined six investment and acquisition decisions of a small computer manufacturer. Based on his field research, Carter offered six modifications to the Cyert and March framework. Most of these modifications are supported by the results of the present research.

First, Carter found that multiple organizational levels influenced goals, expectations, choice, the search process, and organizational learning. The requirement that decisions pass through many levels per se influenced the final decision. The results of the telephone and personal interviews of the present study support this modification. For example, many companies indicated that the factors included and emphasized in foreign investment evaluations changed as the proposal moved up in the organization. The higher the decision, the more important financial criteria became.

Carter's second finding was that rather than a coalition as envisaged by Cyert and March, the organization could be described better by bilateral bargaining throughout the decision process. There is evidence from the present research to support this view. For example, several companies specifically mentioned that the appropriate hurdle rate for a foreign investment is negotiated between the CEO and various groups reviewing the project proposal.

Third, rather than handling uncertainty by use of standard operating rules and a negotiated environment, Carter found that the more uncertain the project, the more criteria by which it would be evaluated. The results of the present study support the finding that companies do not use negotiated environment and standard industry practices extensively to reduce uncertainty. However, tests of the relationship between uncertain projects and the number of criteria used for evaluation were not statistically significant.

Fourth, Carter found that in addition to problem stimulus, search was initiated because of a manager's explicit decisions and in response to opportunities in the operating environment. This result is supported by the findings of the present research. In the telephone and personal interviews, many companies stated that oftentimes the initial suggestion for a foreign investment came from local managers in response to opportunities they observed in their local environment. This result was especially evident when a foreign investment was an acquisition.

Carter also found that projects were evaluated with a basic marginalism rather than discretely. A few firms in the present study indicated that capital constraints forced them to accept only the "best" projects, which implies a basic marginalism in investment analysis. However, the vast majority of companies stated that each project was evaluated on its own merits.

Finally, Carter noted that companies exhibited a "think positive" behavior after a project was accepted. This behavior tended to play down the risks and possible problems of a project that had been brought out in the project analysis. The present research did not evaluate post-acceptance behavior of the sample firms.

The most comprehensive support from the international field for the behavioral theory came from Aharoni's (1966) case study of 38 companies that had considered direct investment in Israel. He studied the organizational factors that influenced foreign investment decisions and the impact of information availability, communication, and use in the decision process. Most of his results support Cyert and March's original formulation of the behavioral framework, and these results are in many cases supported by the present research. For example, Aharoni's finding that companies made decisions in terms of a specific project in a specific country supports Cyert and March's relational concept of problematic search. The results of the current study support this concept as well.

Uncertainty avoidance, a second relational concept of Cyert and March, was found by Aharoni to be a prominent factor in the decision process. Aharoni noted that the initial screening of investments centered around crude risk estimates. Similarly, many companies in the present study stated that the earliest evaluations of a project centered around broad political risk measures.

The importance of organizational expectations in the foreign investment decision process was highlighted by Aharoni in his analysis of the impact of the initiating force on his decision outcome. He found that the variables to be investigated and the scope of the investigation depended largely on the magnitude of the initiating force as well as the perception of the problem by the investigator. This finding has only limited support from the present study. The analysis of responses to the questionnaire indicated no significant relationships between the problem definition and the evaluation methods used. However, the results of the field interviews indicated that the initiator of a project in part determines what factors, e.g., marketing or financial, are dominant in investment analysis.

Although most of Aharoni's findings fit well into the behavioral theory, two findings did not. First, Aharoni found that leadership was an important force in the decision process. The Cyert and March framework with its emphasis on coalitions and organizational slack precluded a role for leadership. The results of the telephone and personal interviews of the present study indicated that the strong backing of an executive plays a critical role in the acceptance of many foreign projects.

Also, Aharoni found that the search for information created commitments which could compel the firm to decide in a certain way. The behavioral theory as outlined by Cyert and March largely ignored commitment. The results of the present study indicated that commitment plays an important role in the decision outcome. For example, several firms stated that lower echelons would not submit a proposal to higher echelons unless they already were committed to the project. Also, they would act to reduce the perceived risk for higher echelons usually by suggesting alternative operating policies.

Finally, Aharoni stressed the importance of information, its cost, availability, and dissemination in the firm as key determinants of the investment decision process. This emphasis on information seems warranted based on the results of the present study. Repeatedly, firms justified their use of qualitative, subjective analyses of overseas risks by emphasizing the worth of information.

Based on his research, Aharoni constructed a variant of the behavioral framework for firm decisions. He retained the relational concepts of Cyert and March: quasi-resolution of conflict, uncertainty avoidance, problematic search, and organizational learning. However, he formulated alternatives to the variables of goals, expectations, and choice. He postulated that the investment decision should be analyzed in terms of (1) structure, (2) participants, (3) interactions, and (4) information (Aharoni, 1966, pp. 292-300). The results of the current study seem to support this reformulation.

In summary, the comparison of the results of the present study to those of earlier research into international investment practices seems to indicate that U.S.-based MNCs are becoming more sophisticated in the financial criteria they use to evaluate foreign investments, e.g., the increased importance of DCF techniques and the use of internal rate of return criteria. The results also indicate an increased emphasis on improved measurement of risk and reflection of risk in the capital-budgeting system, e.g., the use of sensitivity analysis and adjustments to required performance to reflect risks. However, these measurements remain at a fairly judgmental level. Also, the amount of comparative analysis remains limited.

The comparison of the results of the present study to those of recent studies of domestic capital-budgeting trends indicates that companies use similar basic practices domestically and overseas. In both areas, companies seem to be increasing in sophistication in terms of financial criteria used and risk adjustments made. However, the quantification of overseas risks is still highly subjective.

The comparison of results of the present study and those of other studies employing the behavioral framework indicate general agreement. The results of the present study support Aharoni's reformulation of the behavioral framework of Cyert and March.

Comparison of Anticipated and Actual Results of Present Study

The present research was an exploratory field study. Exploratory studies seek what is, and acording to Katz (1953) have three purposes: to discover significant variables in the field situation, to discover relationships between variables, and to lay the groundwork for later, more rigorous testing of hypotheses. The pitfalls of exploratory research is the possibility of chance relationships and improper interpretation of field results. As a guard against these problems, Katz advised clear specification of the broad results the researcher expects to find.

At the outset of the present research several general expectations were elaborated. These expectations derived from two main sources: earlier research in the areas of financial and capital-budgeting practices of MNCs and the behavioral theory of corporate decision-making. The first source led to expectations about relationships between demographic variables and foreign investment evaluation practices. The other source led to expectations about relationships between organizational variables and investment analysis methods. The comparison of actual results with those expected follows next.

Comparison: Actual and Anticipated Results of Demographic Relationships

One of the pioneering investigations into financial practices of MNCs was conducted by Robbins and Stobaugh (1973) as part of the Multinational

Enterprise Project at Harvard. They postulated eight variables to explain financial behavior of multinational enterprises but found that one, foreign sales, was more often correlated with financial practices of MNCs than any other factor.

In a more recent study, Morsicato (1978) researched the foreign performance evaluation practices of U.S. MNCs in the chemical industry. But she found that firm size was not significantly related to performance evaluation practices used.

Based on these results, a preliminary expectation of the current research was that size would be a key discriminator of FDMI practices. Size was measured in terms of total and foreign sales, assets, and income. Foreign sales was found to be related to the other variables and so was used in the subsequent analysis of relationships. Large firms were expected to use more sophisticated evaluation practices than small firms. Sophisticated practices include comparative evaluation of investment opportunities, use of net present value investment criteria, use of discounted cash flow income measures, use of a weighted average cost of capital, and evaluation of investment opportunities in terms of both dollars and local currencies.

Large companies were also expected to use different risk analysis methods than small companies. Large companies were expected to use sophisticated methods such as the use of probability distributions of cash flows, covariance of cash flows with other project cash flows, or sensitivity analysis of cash flows to measure overall risk, foreign currency risk, and political risk; the use of present and future cash flows to assess foreign currency risk; and the use of capital-budgeting procedures that adjust for the unique risks of international operations.

In the present research, three groups of firms, large, medium, and small, were formed. Cross-tabulation tables with chi-square test of significance were used to analyze the relationship between size and investment evaluation practices used. The results of this analysis did not conform to expectations.

Size of the firm showed a statistically significant relationship to only four investment evaluation practices. Small firms tended to rate accounting ROI important as a financial criterion whereas large firms did not. Small firms did not use local cost of debt as a measure of the cost of capital. Large firms did. Small firms dominated in the use of probability distributions to measure political risk and in varying the rate of return required from an investment to adjust for political risk. For all of these relationships, measures of association (Cramer's V) and measures of predictive ability (lambda) were relatively low.

There is one important reason why size might not prove to be a good explanatory variable in the present study. All of the firms in the present study were relatively large companies. For example, the cutoff levels for each group were less than $250 million for the small groups, $250 to $700 million for the

Summary and Conclusions 171

medium group, and greater than $700 million for the large group. In comparison, the three groups in the Morsicato study were less than $100 million dollars for the small group, $100-$500 million for the medium group, and greater than $500 million for the large group. Most of the sample would fall into the medium and large groups of the present study. Thus, the present research may not have captured enough small firms for size to be a good discriminator of evaluation practices used. As discussed earlier, the locus of decision-making and characteristics of the decision itself may also help explain the differences in results.

In addition to size, several other explanatory variables were postulated: *age* of a firm as a multinational, the *importance of a company's foreign operations* (i.e., foreign sales/total sales, foreign assets/total assets, foreign income/total income), the *geographic distribution* of a firm's foreign operations (the number of areas worldwide in which a firm has a FDMI), and the *extensiveness* of a firm's foreign involvement (the number of countries worldwide in which a firm has a FDMI). Old multinationals have greater experience operating internationally and were expected to have developed more sophisticated investment evaluation and risk analysis methods. In companies where foreign operations are an important contributor to total corporate performance, it was expected that more management attention and resources would be devoted to developing sophisticated investment evaluation and risk analysis practices. The same expectation held for companies with extensive and widely dispersed overseas operations.

In order to test for relationships between age and investment evaluation practices, the firms were divided into four groups, multinational since 1950, 1960, 1970, 1978. Cross-tabulations with chi-square tests of significance were used to analyze these relationships. Only four of the relationships were significant, and these did not follow the pattern expected. At an $\alpha = .05$ used for statistical significance in this study, four spurious relationships could result. Without any theoretical basis for the observed pattern of relationships, the results may well be attributed to chance.

As for the demographic variables, the importance of a company's foreign operations was highly related to total foreign sales and so was not analyzed as a separate variable. The two measures of geographic dispersion (distribution and extensiveness of foreign operations) were highly correlated, and so the analysis of relationships was conducted only with the number of areas worldwide where a company had an FDMI.

At the outset high dispersion was expected to be related to the use of sophisticated techniques. It was found that high-dispersion firms view their operations as integrated globally and their practices reflect this focus. Low geographic dispersion showed a significant relationship with the use of parent weighted average cost of capital. High dispersion was related to the use of operational restrictions and discrimination in defining political risk. High dispersion was related to insuring political risks and charging cash flows for these costs. Finally, high dispersion was related to the use of sensitivity analysis to measure foreign currency risks.

The last set of demographic variables tested for relationships with foreign evaluation practices was the geographic area in which a company made its most recent FDMI. A recent study by Bavishi (1979) had found the MNCs analyzed investments in LDCs differently than those in DCs. A similar result was anticipated and found for the present study.

Investment in Europe, Latin America, Asia and the Far East showed statistically significant relationships with more evaluation practices than any other demographic variables. Companies investing in Europe tended to use more sophisticated practices than companies investing in Latin America. For example, companies investing in Europe were less concerned with funds available for repatriation to the parent than other firms; i.e., they tended to take a local perspective on investment evaluation. They also used more sophisticated measures of business and political risk, relying heavily on probability calculations. These findings probably reflect the greater availability and reliability of data in DCs and the concurrent willingness of executives to develop probability estimates.

The results of the statistical analysis are supported by the findings of the telephone and personal interviews. Most companies indicated that they favored qualitative analysis in LDCs because of the lack of reliable information. They were more likely to use quantitiative evaluations in DCs where they felt more comfortable with projecting cash flows and assigning probabilities to future events.

Overall, three demographic variables were found in the present study to deserve attention in future research: size of the firm, dispersion of investment, and geographic area of investment. Of these, area of investment appears to have the greatest potential for explaining the evaluation practices companies use. An important area for further investigation is the difference in practices individual firms use to evaluate opportunities in various parts of the world.

Comparison: Actual and Anticipated Results of Behavioral Relationships

The anticipated findings described so far relate to relationships between demographic variables and companies' investment evaluation and risk analysis practices. Based on the behavioral theory of firm decision-making, several other results were anticipated. First, the behavioral theory postulates that firms seek to satisfy multiple objectives (as opposed to a single profit-maximizing goal). Thus, it was expected that FDMI evaluation would be subject to several objectives. This expectation was supported by the actual results. Although most companies had a profit goal for direct investments, they also had sales and growth objectives as well.

As indicated earlier, Aharoni (1966) found in his investigations of foreign investment decision behavior that the decision-maker strongly influenced the type and scope of investigation into an investment opportunity. Thus, it was anticipated that the decision-maker would be an important discriminatory variable. Consistent with Aharoni's findings, it was expected that the higher up in the corporate structure the decision-maker is, the more sophisticated the evaluation procedures and risk analysis methods employed.

The analysis of responses to the questionnaire did not uncover any significant relationships between the decision-maker and evaluation practices used. However, the results of the telephone and personal interviews indicated that subtle changes in evaluation practices occur as a project moves up in the corporate hierarchy, with top management emphasizing financial criteria.

Third, the behavioral theory emphasizes that the firm is a coalition of subgroups (rather than a single unit with one goal). Thus, the behavioral theory approach views the organizational structure of a company as a key variable in the analysis of firm decision-making. How companies are organized globally was expected to help explain the type of investment evaluation and risk analysis methods they employ. Davis (1976) has described the evolution of multinational corporate organization as moving from no international organization, to international division, to either a geographic product or functional organization internationally, to, finally, a matrix structure. It was expected that companies exhibiting a matrix, geographic, functional, or product organization would employ more sophisticated techniques for investment evaluation and risk analysis than companies with no international organization or an international division.

To test for relationships between organizational structure and evaluation practices, five groups were created and cross-tabulation analysis was undertaken. Only two significant relationships were found. On this basis, organizational structure was not found to be a good explanatory variable. However, the results of the personal and telephone interviews provided some support for the importance of organizational structure. For example, the source of the investment proposal, the factors analyzed, and the criteria stressed in the evaluation process differed between companies organized geographically and those organized in global product lines.

Fourth, according to the behavioral theory, search for the solution to a problem is limited. Several studies have found that decision behavior is not characterized by a search for the "best" solution. Rather, search is made to find the first feasible alternative to solve a problem. Thus, it was expected that corporate behavior with respect to FDMI evaluation would be characterized by go-no go decisions on specific opportunities, rather than by comparative analysis. This expectation was confirmed by the actual results. Seventy-one percent of the respondents to the questionnaire stated that they did not use comparative analysis for foreign investments.

Not only is search limited, it is also biased. Aharoni (1966) found that how a problem is defined affects the factors considered in seeking a solution. Thus, problem definition (in this research, the motive for investing overseas) was expected to be related to the evaluation methods employed for analyzing a specific FDMI. The cross-tabulation analysis of survey responses indicated that no significant relationships existed.

The behavioral theory postulates that decision-making is characterized by uncertainty avoidance. Cyert and March (1962) found that corporations sought to avoid risk in decision-making by following industry tradition. It was expected that companies in the same industry would use similar investment evaluation and risk analysis methods. Further, Carter (1969) found that the more uncertain the environment, the greater the number of criteria on which an investment was evaluated. It was expected that companies whose most recent FDMI was made outside the industry of the parent would subject that decision to a greater number and more sophisticated evaluation methods than companies who invest overseas in their own industry.

A cross-tabulation analysis was undertaken between all industry groups and the investment evaluation practices used. The number of significant relationships was small enough to have been due to chance. Thus, standard industry practices do not appear to prevail.

In order to test Carter's result, the evaluation practices of companies investing in their own industry overseas were compared to those of companies investing outside their industry. The assumption was that investment in another industry would be viewed as riskier than investment in the parent's industry. The cross-tabulation analysis indicated no significant relationships between industry of investment and either the specific type or number of practices used. It may be that although companies invested outside their primary parent industry, they were still making an investment in an industry in which they already had a domestic operation. So the overseas investment may not have been viewed as a more uncertain one than in the primary industry.

Cyert and March (1962) also found that companies seek to avoid uncertainty in decision-making by utilizing standard operating procedures. This implies that standard procedures would be used to evaluate investment opportunities worldwide. It was expected that any changes noted in FDMI evaluation practices should be due to changes in practices over time, rather than changes to reflect specific characteristics of the investment opportunity (geographic area, etc.). However, the behavioral theory also stresses that organizations learn. Firms learn what aspects of the environment to pay attention to through experience. So the expected result stated above applied only to the subgroup of companies that had not experienced foreign currency or political-related losses in the past 10 years. Companies with foreign currency losses were expected to use sophisticated foreign currency risk assessment methods. Companies with losses due to changes in the political environment should have used sophisticated political risk assessment techniques.

The use of standard operating policies to avoid uncertainty was supported by the actual results. The paired t-test analysis of changes in evaluation practices indicated that corporate policies change little over time. The responses to the questionnaire indicated that these changes result from improvements in standard company practices rather than from unique analyses of particular investments. However, the analysis of demographic variables indicated that the geographic area of investment showed significant relationships with evaluation practices used. Thus, the sensitivity of evaluation practices within individual companies to geographic differences should be explored in more detail in future research.

The importance of learning in the investment decision process was supported by two findings of the present research. First, companies appeared to learn from past experience what risks to consider most important in investment evaluation. Based on risk ratings for their most recent FDMI, companies were found to use different evaluation practices.

Similarly, loss record due to political or currency risks impacted the evaluation practices used. For political losses the expected pattern was paralleled by actual results. Companies which had suffered negative effects due to political changes overseas dominated in the use of sophisticated political risk definition and measurement. Although the record of currency losses was significantly related to several evaluation practices, none were in the definition, measurement, or adjustment for currency risk.

The results of the telephone and personal interviews also support the importance of organizational learning in the decision process. The history of losses was found to be a determinant of the factors stressed in the qualitative analysis of investment proposals.

Overall, the results of the present study largely conformed to expectations derived from the behavioral theory. In several cases, the analysis of responses to the questionnaire did not seem to support the anticipated outcomes, but subsequent field research supported the behavioral approach. It is possible that a questionnaire approach, while valid for documenting current practices and discovering general relationships, was not sensitive enough to discern the intricacies of the decision process. Thus, the personal field interviews provided invaluable perspective on the relationships in the decision process.

This finding should be considered in developing methodologies for analyzing corporate decisions in future research.

Summary of Comparisons

Comparisons of the present results with those of earlier studies of international investment decision-making of MNCs indicated that firms are moving toward use of more sophisticated evaluation criteria and risk measurement techniques. However, the practices used by the majority of firms today are at a basic level when compared to the methods advocated by normative theories. This is especially true in the area of foreign risk measurement and in the reflection of risk in capital-budgeting procedures. The primary limitations to adopting more sophisticated techniques uncovered in this research were lack of top-management understanding of the techniques and lack of adequate information necessary for the more sophisticated methods. The combination of these factors results in a feeling of personal risk and so a reluctance for executives to adopt more sophisticated techniques.

Comparing the results of the present study to those of recent research into domestic capital-budgeting practices indicated that firms tended to use similar methods of analysis worldwide. Again, the trend seems to be toward adoption of more sophisticated financial criteria for evaluation, but risk analysis remains at a fundamental level.

Comparison of the results of the present research to those applying the behavioral framework indicated broad agreement in the findings. The main area of disagreement is in how firms dealt with uncertainty in the decision process. However, the key variables and relational concepts of the behavioral theory were generally supported by the findings of the present research.

A comparison of the actual and anticipated results for numerous demographic variables uncovered two variables with significant relationships to evaluation practices used, geographic dispersion of a firm's operations and geographic area of investment. Area of investment proved to be the most important explanatory variable reflecting the division for analytical purposes that companies make between investing in LDCs versus DCs.

Finally, a comparison of the anticipated results based on the behavior of framework and the actual results indicated broad consistency with the behavioral approach. This is especially true for the results of the personal and telephone interviews. The findings of the current research support the modifications proposed by Aharoni to the original behavioral model of Cyert and March. Aharoni's emphasis on commitment and the crucial role of information in the decision process seems warranted based on the present findings.

Future Research

The nature of the present research is inductive, and as such it is intended as an initial step in the process of theory development. This study should provide a basis for numerous future research efforts.

First, one of the aims of this research was to gain insight into the reasons companies make foreign direct investments. It was hoped that an improved understanding of these reasons would give some perspective on which of several scenarios (e.g., the Hufbauer and Adler classical, reverse classical, or anticlassical cases) best described corporate foreign investment behavior. The results of the mail questionnaire in the present research were evenly split between defensive and aggressive motives for investment so that no clearcut support for any one scenario was found. However, during the personal interviews, it became clear that an analysis of the competitive environment is a standard component of any foreign project proposal. Thus, the field analysis of these proposals would be a useful methodology for future research in this area.

Second, at the outset of this study six major theories of direct foreign investment at the aggregate level were outlined. It was emphasized that empirical tests of these theories did not give clearcut support to any single theory as an explanation of foreign investment behavior of MNCs. The results of the present study indicate that theories grounded in classical economic assumptions (e.g., profit maximization as a guide to decision behavior, conditions of certainty or knowledge of probability distributions, etc.) will prove to have limited ability to explain investment behavior. Based on the outcome of the present research, an important area of future research should be the development of a positive theory of direct investment on the behavioral theory approach. Key elements of the theory would include uncertainty resolution, commitments, and information.

Third, the results of the present study indicate that the actual investment evaluation practices used by the majority of U.S. MNCs are much less sophisticated that those advocated in normative theories. As many authors have noted, it is important for normative theories to prescribe attainable goals based on realistic conditions. A crucial area for future research would be the development of models guiding firms on how to reflect measured risks into the capital-budgeting system. These models should take into account the limited and costly information available to firms and the risk measurements companies actually use.

The results of the current research indicate that once corporate evaluation practices are adopted, they tend to remain in effect. Even in the face of direct losses, the actual evaluation practices used do not change much. In light of the limited acceptance of some of the more sophisticated practices of risk analysis advocated in normative research, one promising area for future research would be a study of the factors influencing practice adoption and change.

As a result of the present study, several variables were uncovered that had significant relationships with foreign investment evaluation practices. Several avenues for future research came from these findings. An important study would be an analysis of the relative importance of the various factors in determining the evaluation practices used. For example, what are the relative weights companies attach to the geographic area of investment and the past loss history in choosing evaluation practices for a given investment?

In addition, the significant variables discovered in the present study were not found to have a strong predictive relationship to evaluation practices. An area for future research would be the discovery of variables to predict what practices companies use. The findings of such research would provide a basis for a predictive model of direct-investment patterns. Based on the present research, the geographic area of investment should be a good factor to begin analyzing in such research. The division in the ways that firms view investments in LDCs and DCs, and also the differences in the ways they analyze such investments, exists today and has since the earliest studies on foreign investment evaluation.

Finally, the current results indicate that standard evaluation practices are applied with a fair degree of uniformity worldwide. Thus, the evaluation process seems to ignore some of the unique aspects of different environments although most executives interviewed felt that the evaluation system should reflect such differences. An important area for future research would be a study focused on the specific differences in practices companies actually use to evaluate domestic versus foreign investments and investments in diverse foreign environments.

Appendix A

Companies Included in Present Survey and Harvard Multinational Enterprise Study

Table 78

List of Companies in the Sample

Abbott Laboratories (209)[a]
Addressograph Multigraph Corporation (334)
Adolph Coors Company (321)
Agway, Inc. (162)
Allied Chemicals (82)
Allis Chalmers (146)
Alumax, Inc. (352)
Aluminum Co. of America (72)
American Can (64)
American Cyanamid (107)
American Home Products (89)
American Motors (94)
American Standard (134)
AMF (201)
AMP, Inc. (356)
Armco Steel Corporation (63)
Armstrong Cork Company (230)
A-T-O Inc. (357)
Avco Corporation (305)
Avery International (463)
Avon Products, Inc. (157)

Bausch & Lomb, Inc. (475)
Baxter Travenol Laboratories, Inc. (294)
Beatrice Foods (38)
Becton, Dickenson & Company (367)
Bell & Howell Company (391)
Bemis Company, Inc. (315)
Bendix Corporation (70)
Bethlehem Steel (33)

Black & Decker Manufacturing Company (276)
Blue Bell, Inc. (281)
Boeing Company (47)
Boise Cascade (116)
Borden, Inc. (59)
Borg Warner (121)
Bristol-Myers Company (113)
Brunswick Corporation (247)
Bucyrus-Erie Company (379)
Budd Company (215)
Burlington Industries Inc. (98)
Burroughs (120)

Cabot Corporation (389)
Cameron Iron Works Inc. (422)
Campbell Soup (136)
Carnation (103)
Carrier Corporation (199)
Caterpillar Tractor (36)
Celanese (106)
Central Soya Co., Inc. (124)
C. F. Industries (51)
Champion Spark Plug Company (362)
Chesebrough-Pond's, Inc. (277)
Chicago Bridge & Iron Co. (331)
Chrysler (10)
Cincinnati Milacron, Inc. (398)
Clark Equipment Co. (180)
Cluett, Peabody & Co., Inc. (330)
Coca Cola Company (69)

Table 78 (Continued)

Colgate Palmolive (54)
Colt Industries (178)
Combustion Engineering (125)
Consolidated Foods (78)
Continental Group (56)
Control Data (173)
Corning Glass Works (219)
C P C International (79)
Crane Company (208)
Crown Cork & Seal (248)
Cummins Engine Co., Inc. (218)
Cutler-Hammer Inc. (401)

Dana (155)
Dart Industries (152)
Deere & Company (66)
Del Monte (158)
Diamond Shamrock (167)
Digital Equipment Corp. (280)
Dow Chemical Co. (25)
Dow Corning Corp. (471)
Dresser Industries, Inc. (101)

Eastman Kodak (28)
Eaton Corp. (127)
Economics Laboratories, Inc. (494)
E. I. duPont de Nemours (16)
Eli Lilly & Co. (171)
Eltra Corporation (265)
Emerson Electric Company (147)
Emhart Corporation (202)

Envirotech Corp. (424)
Esmark, Inc. (32)

Fairchild Camera & Instrument Corp. (404)
Federal Mogul (412)
Ferro Corporation (451)
Firestone Tire & Rubber (46)
FMC (97)
Ford Motor (3)
Foxboro Company (500)
Frederick & Herrud, Inc. (469)
Freuhauf (153)

GAF (216)
Gardner Denver Co. (403)
General Dynamics (85)
General Electric (9)
General Foods (44)
General Instrument Corp. (443)
General Mills (81)
General Motors Corp. (2)
General Signal Corp. (312)
General Tire & Rubber (111)
Genesco, Inc. (196)
Gillette Co. (150)
Gold Kist Inc. (251)
B. F. Goodrich (112)
Goodyear Tire & Rubber (23)
Gould, Inc. (185)
W. R. Grace (50)

Table 78 (Continued)

Hercules, Inc. (142)
Hewlett-Packard Co. (200)
H. K. Porter Co., Inc. (466)
H. J. Heinz (119)
Hobart (415)
Honeywell (88)
Hoover Co. (335)
Hoover Universal, Inc. (499)
H. P. Hood, Inc. (417)
Hughes Tool Company (448)
Hyster Co. (454)

IBM (8)
Idle Wild Foods, Inc. (495)
Ingersoll-Rand (117)
Interlake, Inc. (289)
International Harvester (27)
International Paper (52)
International Telephone & Telegraph (11)

Johns-Manville (174)
Johnson & Johnson (87)
Joseph E. Seagrams & Sons (241)
Joy Manufacturing Co. (302)

Kaiser Aluminum & Chemical Corp. (122)
Kellogg (163)
Kimberly-Clark (143)
Koehring Co. (470)
Koppers Co., Inc. (190)
Kraft, Inc. (37)

Land O'Lakes, Inc. (183)
Lear Siegler, Inc. (292)
Levi Straus (186)
Libbey-Owens-Ford Co. (253)
Liggitt Group, Inc. (283)
Litton Industries (60)
Lockheed Aircraft (61)
Lubrizoil Corp. (395)
Lykes (140)

Macmillan Co. (376)
Martin Marietta Corp. (189)
Masco Corporation (420)
Mattel, Inc. (486)
McGraw-Hill, Inc. (323)
Mead Corp. (141)
Memorex Corp. (481)
Merck & Co., Inc. (132)
Midland-Ross Corporation (425)
Miles Laboratories (397)
Minnesota Mining & Manufacturing (53)
Monsanto (42)
Motorola, Inc. (149)

Nabisco (110)
Nalco Chemical Corp. (447)
National Can Corp. (246)
National Distillers & Chemical Corp. (193)
National Starch & Chemical Corp. (487)
NCR (96)
New York Times Company (394)

Table 78 (Continued)

NL Industries (175)
Northrop Corp. (179)
Norton Company (303)
Norton Simon Inc. (131)

Olin Corp. (164)
Owens-Corning Fiberglass (210)
Owens-Illinois (84)

Pabst Brewing Company (319)
Paccar, Inc. (227)
Parker-Hannifin Corp. (429)
Peavy Co. (369)
Pennwalt Corporation (272)
Pepsico, Inc. (77)
Perkin-Elmer Corporation (473)
Pfizer, Inc. (118)
Philip Morris, Inc. (65)
Pillsbury Co. (159)
Pitney-Bowes, Inc. (347)
Polaroid Corporation (239)
PPG Industries, Inc. (100)
Proctor & Gamble (19)

Quaker Oats (154)
Questor Corporation (406)

Ralston Purina (58)
Raytheon (90)
RCA (31)
Reichhold Chemicals, Inc. (325)

Reliance Electric Co. (298)
Revlon, Inc. (235)
Reynolds Metals (108)
Richardson-Merrell, Inc. (279)
R. J. Reynolds Industries (41)
Rockwell International (34)
Rohm & Haas (195)

St. Regis Paper (135)
Schering-Plough Corp. (254)
SCM (172)
Scott Paper (166)
Scovill Manufacturing Co. (301)
G. D. Searle & Co. (273)
Sherwin-Williams Co. (238)
Signode Corp. (402)
Simmons Company (387)
Singer (105)
SmithKline Corp. (296)
Sperry Rand (62)
Square D. Company (353)
Squibb Corporation (188)
Standard Brands, Inc. (126)
Stanley Works (339)
Stauffer Chemical Co. (204)
Sterling Drug, Inc. (205)
Studebaker-Worthington (187)
Sunbeam Corporation (236)
Sybron Corporation (332)

Table 78 (Continued)

Tecumseh Products Co. (333)
Tektronix Inc. (457)
Tenneco (20)
Texas Instruments, Inc. (133)
Textron (83)
Time, Inc. (217)
Timken Co. (253)
Trane Corporation (409)
TRW (71)

Union Carbide (21)
Uniroyal (95)
United Merchants & Manufacturers, Inc. (207)
U.S. Filter Corporation (465)
U.S. Gypsum Company (233)
U.S. Industries, Inc. (109)

U.S. Steel (14)
United Technologies (35)
Upjohn Company (220)

Varian Associates (485)

Walter Kidde & Co., Inc. (184)
Warner Lambert (93)
Washington Post Company (452)
Westinghouse Electric (22)
Wheelabrator-Frye Inc. (434)
White Motor Corporation (168)
Willamette Industries (345)
Wm. Wrigley, Jr. Co. (456)

Xerox (40)

[a]Numbers in parentheses denote 1977 Fortune 500 rank.

Table 79

List of Companies in 1975 Harvard Multinational Enterprise Project Sample

Abbott Laboratories
Addressograph Multigraph Corporation
Allied Chemical Corporation
Allis-Chalmers Corporation
Aluminium Company of America
American Can Company
American Cyanamid Company
American Home Products Corporation
AMF Incorporated
AMAX, Inc.
ASARCO Incorporated
American Standard Inc.
Archer Daniels Midland Company
Armco Steel Corporation
Armstrong Cork Company

Beatrice Foods Company
Bendix Corporation
Black and Decker Manufacturing Company
Borden, Inc.
Borg-Warner Corporation
Bristol-Myers Company
Brunswick Corporation
Budd Company
Burlington Industries, Inc.

Cabot Corporation
Campbell Soup Company
Carborundum Company
Carnation Company
Caterpillar Tractor Company

Celanese Corporation
Champion Spark Plug Company
Chemetron Corporation
Chesebrough-Pond's Inc.
Chicago Pneumatic Tool Company
Chrysler Corporation
Cities Service Company
Clark Equipment Company
Coca-Cola Company
Colgate-Palmolive Company
Combustion Engineering, Inc.
Continental Can Company, Inc.
Continental Oil Company
Corning Glass Works
CPC International Inc.
Crane Co.
Crown Cork & Seal Company, Inc.

Dana Corporation
Deere & Company
Del Monte Corporation
Dow Chemical Co.
Dresser Industries, Inc.

E. I. duPont de Nemours & Company
Eli Lilly and Company
ESB Incorporated
Eastman Kodak Company
Eaton Corporation
Eltra Corporation
Emhart Corporation

Table 79 (Continued)

Englehard Minerals & Chemicals Corporation
Esmark, Inc.
Exxon Corporation

FMC Corporation
Federal-Mogul Corporation
Firestone Tire & Rubber Company
Ford Motor Company
Foremost-McKesson, Inc.
Fruehauf Corporation

GATX Corporation
General Dynamics Corporation
General Electric Company
General Foods Corporation
General Mills, Inc.
General Motors Corporation
General Telephone & Electronics Corp.
General Tire & Rubber Company
Genesco Inc.
The Gillette Company
B. F. Goodrich Company
Goodyear Tire & Rubber Company
Gould Inc.
W. R. Grace & Co.
Greyhound Corporation
Gulf Oil Corporation

H. J. Heinz Company
Hercules Incorporated
Hobart Corporation
Honeywell Inc.

Hoover Company
Hygrade Food Products Corporation

IC Industries, Inc.
Ingersoll-Rand Company
Inmont Corporation
International Business Machines Corp.
International Harvester Company
International Paper Company
International Telephone and Telegraph Corp.

Johns-Manville Corporation
Johnson & Johnson
JOY Manufacturing Company

Kaiser Industries Corporation
Kellogg Company
Kimberly-Clark Corporation
Koppers Company, Incorporated
Kraftco Corporation

Litton Industries, Inc.
Lockheed Aircraft Corporation

P. R. Mallory & Co., Inc.
Marcor Inc.
Maremont Corporation
Martin Marietta Corporation
Merck & Co., Inc.
Miles Laboratories, Inc.
Minnesota Mining and Manufacturing Co.
Mobil Oil Corporation

Table 79 (Continued)

Monsanto Company

Nabisco, Inc.
NCR Corporation
National Distillers & Chemical Corp.
NL Industries, Inc.
Norton Company

Olin Corporation
Otis Elevator Company
Owens-Corning Fiberglas Corporation
Owens-Illinois, Inc.

PPG Industries, Inc.
Pennwalt Corporation
PepsiCo Inc.
Pet Incorporated
Pfizer Inc.
Phelps Dodge Corporation
Philip Morris Incorporated
Phillips Petroleum Company
Pillsbury Company
H. K. Porter Company, Inc.
Procter & Gamble Company
Purex Corporation

Quaker Oats Company

RCA Corporation
Ralston Purina Company
Rapid-American Corporation

Raytheon Company
Revlon, Inc.
Reynolds Metals Company
Richardson-Merrell Inc.
H. H. Robertson Company
Rockwell International Corporation
Rohm and Haas Company

Schering-Plough Corporation
SCM Corporation
St. Regis Paper Company
Scott Paper Company
Scovill Manufacturing Company
Simmons Company
Singer Company
SmithKline Corporation
Sperry Rand Corporation
Squibb Corporation
A. E. Staley Manufacturing Company
Standard Brands Incorporated
Standard Oil Company of California
Standard Oil Company (Indiana)
Stauffer Chemical Company
Sterling Drug, Inc.
Studebaker-Worthington, Inc.
Sunbeam Corporation

TRW Inc.
Texaco, Inc.
Texas Instruments Incorporated
Time Incorporated
Timken Company

Table 79 (Continued)

USM Corporation	Warner-Lambert Company
Union Carbide Corporation	Westinghouse Electric Corporation
UNIROYAL, Inc.	Weyerhaeuser Company
United Merchants and Manufacturers, Inc.	Wm. Wrigley Jr. Company
Upjohn Company	
UV Industries, Inc.	

Appendix B

Cover Letter and Questionnaire Used in Present Survey Research

THE PENNSYLVANIA STATE UNIVERSITY

509 BUSINESS ADMINISTRATION BUILDING
UNIVERSITY PARK, PENNSYLVANIA 16802

College of Business Administration
Department of Business Logistics

May 14, 1979

Dear

This letter invites your company to participate in a study of multinational enterprise investment evaluation methods. The objective of this research project is to gain a better understanding of the techniques used by multinational companies to analyze foreign investment opportunities in order to recommend improvements based on current practice. I am a Ph.D. candidate in international finance at The Pennsylvania State University and this research is an integral part of my doctoral dissertation.

In recent years the operating environment for multinational companies has changed rapidly, due in part to developments such as floating exchange rates, challenges to the dollar, worldwide stagflation, FASB #8, etc. This study focuses on the international investment procedures used by multinationals to cope with such developments. The research will document the methods which are used by the top management of multinational enterprises to evaluate the business, foreign currency and political risks of overseas investment opportunities.

As a result of this project, recommendations for multinational enterprise policy decisions on international investment analysis which are based on practical applications will be developed. Thus it is necessary to have the cooperation of experienced members of the business community. The participation of your firm is of great importance to this research effort.

Participation will give your company the opportunity to learn more about the foreign investment evaluation practices used by other U.S. multinational companies. If you would like to receive a summary of the results obtained from this study, please complete the form on the first page of the questionnaire.

I would appreciate it if you would take a few minutes to complete the enclosed questionnaire or route it to the most appropriate individual in your organization. A number identifying your company appears in the upper right-hand corner of the questionnaire. Any information provided will be kept strictly confidential. It is only necessary for me to know what companies and individuals have participated for follow-up interviews when appropriate.

If you have any questions, feel free to contact me [(814) 865-1269]. May I please hear from you soon?

                                            Sincerely yours,

                                            Marie E. Wicks
                                            Instructor in
                                            International Business

MEW/mrf

Enclosure

SURVEY OF FOREIGN DIRECT-INVESTMENT
DECISIONS OF MULTINATIONAL CORPORATIONS

The purpose of this survey is to explore the foreign direct-investment decisions of U.S.-based multinational corporations. Specifically, it seeks to understand what factors motivate direct investment in various areas of the world, how major U.S. multinational corporations evaluate foreign investment opportunities, and how these companies analyze the unique risks inherent in international operations.

The survey includes 30 questions and is divided into four sections:

1. Foreign Investment Evaluation Practices

2. International Risk Analysis Methods

3. Company Information

4. Comments

If you would like to receive a copy of the results of this investigation, please fill in the following information and return it with your completed questionnaire.

Name and Title: _____

Company: _____

Address: _____

_____

GENERAL INSTRUCTIONS

1. This survey seeks information on the investment evaluation methods of U.S.-based multinational companies making <u>foreign direct investments in manufacturing operations</u>. For the purpose of this research, a foreign direct investment means that (a) the multinational company obtains at least 25% of the equity of a new or existing foreign operation; (b) the 25% share is acquired at the time of the initial investment in the foreign affiliate; (c) the 25% share includes equity participation directly from the parent company and also indirectly via other foreign affiliates. If your company's share of an affiliate was less than 25% at the time of investment or if the affiliate was not engaged in manufacturing as its primary activity, please do not provide information on that affiliate.

2. The survey asks for information on your company's <u>most recent</u> foreign direct manufacturing investment (FDMI). If more than one investment was made in the same year, please respond for your largest investment in that year.

3. For the purposes of this study, it is important to obtain information on your company's <u>actual</u> foreign investment decision-making practices for its most recent FDMI and also to understand how these might differ from your standard corporate practices used today. So in many cases, questions are asked regarding your company's practices (1) at the time of investment for the most recent FDMI and (2) today for a <u>typical</u> potential FDMI. Please answer part (2) for your company's most common practices for a typical FDMI today (typical in terms of size, activity, and geographic location).

4. If for any reason you do not complete the entire questionnaire, please return it anyway. Even partial information provides important input to the survey results.

5. Again, all individual responses will be kept strictly confidential. Thus, I hope you will be completely candid.

THANK YOU FOR YOUR SUPPORT OF THIS RESEARCH EFFORT.

SURVEY OF FOREIGN DIRECT-INVESTMENT
DECISIONS OF MULTINATIONAL CORPORATIONS

Did your company have at least 25 percent ownership of a <u>manufacturing</u> facility in 6 or more countries in the following years?

		Yes	No
(a)	1978	☐	☐
(b)	1970	☐	☐
(c)	1960	☐	☐
(d)	1950	☐	☐

If you answered No to (a) above, please fill out question 6 in Section IV and return the questionnaire without further completion.

Section I: Foreign Investment Evaluation Practices

The questions in this section seek to determine why companies invest in various parts of the world and what method(s) they use to evaluate international investment opportunities.

General Objective of Foreign Investment

1. Below are listed five possible objectives for foreign investments. Please check (✓) which objective (1) was important for your company's most recent FDMI and (2) is important for a typical potential FDMI today. You may check more than one objective but please place a 1 next to the most important objective in the investment decision.

	Most Recent FDMI	FDMI Today	
(a)			Increase market share
(b)			Increase growth
(c)			Increase profits
(d)			Decrease production costs
(e)			Decrease risk through geographic diversification

Specific Reasons for Foreign Investment

2. Below are listed more specific reasons for undertaking a foreign investment. Please check (✓) the most important reason(s) (1) at the time of investment for your company's most recent FDMI and (2) for a typical potential FDMI today.

	Most Recent FDMI	FDMI Today	
(a)			Gain economies of scale
(b)			Lower wage costs
(c)			Respond to government pressure to produce locally
(d)			Take advantage of government incentives
(e)			Overcome tariff barriers
(f)			Follow customer
(g)			Fear of losing export market
(h)			Other, please specify (1) _____ _____ (most recent) (2) _____ _____ (today)

Decision Maker for Foreign Investment

3. In the investment decision procedure it is possible that different individuals may initiate an investment proposal, make the investment decision, and approve that decision. Please check who in your organization (1) <u>actually made the decision</u> to invest for the most recent FDMI and (2) <u>would make that decision</u> for a typical potential FDMI today. You may check more than one.

	Board of Directors	Headquarters CEO	Headquarters CFO	Area Manager	Regional Staff	Local Staff	Other: Please Specify
Most Recent FDMI							
FDMI Today							
	(a)	(b)	(c)	(d)	(e)	(f)	(g)

Comparative Analysis of Foreign Investments

4. In making an investment decision, please check which one of the following statements best describes your company's (1) actual approach at the time of investment for the most recent FDMI and (2) approach today for a typical potential FDMI.

	Most Recent FDMI	FDMI Today	
(a)			Each investment is analyzed separately and a go-no go decision is made.
(b)			An investment is compared with a limited number of other alternatives in the same geographic area and the best project is accepted.
(c)			An investment is compared with a limited number of other alternatives of the same type in all geographic areas and the best project is accepted.
(d)			All investments available to the firm worldwide are compared.
(e)			Other, please specify (1) _____ _____ (most recent) (2) _____ _____ (today)

Financial Criteria for Foreign Investment

5. Below are six financial criteria for evaluating investments. Please rate these in order of importance (1) at the time of investment for the most recent FDMI and (2) today for a typical potential FDMI. Rating: 1 (not important) to 5 (very important).

	Most Recent FDMI	FDMI Today	
(a)			Payback
(b)			Accounting Return on Investment
(c)			Return on Sales
(d)			Internal Rate of Return
(e)			Net Present Value
(f)			Contribution to EPS

Measure of Income from Foreign Investment

6. Below are listed several measures of potential income (e.g., dividends, reinvested earnings, licensing fees, etc.) from a foreign investment. Please check which measure(s) your company (1) actually used at the time of investment to analyze its most recent FDMI and (2) uses to analyze a typical potential FDMI today.

	Most Recent FDMI	FDMI Today	
(a)			All earnings after foreign taxes
(b)			All earnings after foreign taxes available for repatriation.
(c)			All cash inflows to the parent, after foreign and domestic taxes.
(d)			All cash inflows to parent, plus reinvested earnings adjusted for foreign and domestic taxes.
(e)			All cash inflows to the parent, plus reinvested earnings adjusted for foreign taxes only.
(f)			Other, please specify (1) _____ _____(most recent) (2) _____ _____(today)

Measure of Investment for Foreign Opportunities

7. Below are listed several measures of the amount of investment in a foreign affiliate. Please check which measure(s) your company (1) actually used at the time of investment to analyze its most recent FDMI and (2) uses today to analyze a typical potential FDMI.

	Most Recent FDMI	FDMI Today	
(a)			Affiliate Total Assets
(b)			Affiliate Total Capital Employed
(c)			Affiliate Net Worth

	Most Recent FDMI	FDMI Today	
(d)			Parent Net Contributions (parent share of equity capital plus loans and advances)
(e)			Purchase Price
(f)			Other, please specify (1) _____ (most recent) _____ (2) _____ (today)

Definition of Cost of Capital for Foreign Investment

8a. If your company uses a discounted cash flow method to evaluate foreign investments, please check which definition(s) of the cost of capital your company (1) used at the time of investment to analyze its most recent FDMI and (2) uses today to analyze a typical potential FDMI.

	Parent			Local			
	Cost of Debt	Cost of Equity	Weighted Average	Cost of Debt	Cost of Equity	Weighted Average	Other
Most Recent FDMI							
FDMI Today							
	(a)	(b)	(c)	(d)	(e)	(f)	(g)

b. If you checked <u>other</u> above, please describe your company's definition(s) of the cost of capital. (1) _____
_____ (Most Recent FDMI)
_____ (2) _____
_____ (FDMI Today)

Section II: International Risk Analysis

The questions in this section seek to determine how multinational corporations analyze the unique risks of foreign operations, specifically foreign currency and political risk.

1. Please rank the following risks in order of importance for the country of your company's most recent FDMI (at the time of investment). Ranking: 1 (least important) to 3 (most important).

    (a) ☐ Business Risk (i.e., commercial, competitive, etc.)

    (b) ☐ Currency Risk

    (c) ☐ Political Risk

Measure of Business Risk

2. Below are listed six methods for measuring business risk. Please check (✓) which method(s) your company (1) actually used at the time of investment to analyze its most recent FDMI and (2) uses today to analyze a typical potential FDMI.

	Most Recent FDMI	FDMI Today	
(a)			Make a subjective evaluation of risk.
(b)			Project a probability distribution of cash flows.
(c)			Estimate the covariance of cash flows with other investment cash flows.
(d)			Perform a sensitivity analysis.
(e)			Calculate the probability of loss.
(f)			Make no risk assessment.
(g)			Other, please specify (1) _____ _____ (most recent) (2) _____ _____ (today)

Adjustment for Business Risk

3. Once the degree of business risk from investment has been measured there are several adjustments that might be made in capital-budgeting procedures to account for risk. Please check which method(s) your company (1) actually used at the time of investment to account for risk in analyzing its most recent FDMI and (2) uses today in analyzing a typical potential FDMI.

	Most Recent FDMI	FDMI Today	
(a)			Vary rate of return required from the FDMI.
(b)			Vary cost of capital used in discounted cash flow analysis.
(c)			Vary payback period required from the FDMI.
(d)			Insure risks and charge cash flows for these costs.
(e)			Charge cash flows for cost of insuring risks even if not taken.
(f)			Make no adjustment for risk.
(g)			Other, please specify (1) _____ (most recent) (2) _____ (today)

Definition of Political Risk

4. Please check (√) the definition(s) of political risk that your company (1) used at the time of investment for analyzing its most recent FDMI and (2) uses today to analyze a typical potential FDMI.

	Most Recent FDMI	FDMI Today	
(a)			Expropriation or nationalization.
(b)			Restrictions on repatriations to parent (e.g., dividends, royalties, capital, etc.)

	Most Recent FDMI	FDMI Today
(c)		
(d)		
(e)		
(f)		

(c) Operational restrictions (e.g., ownership, employment policies, market share, etc.).

(d) Breaches or unilateral changes in contracts and agreements.

(e) Discrimination (e.g., excessive taxation, requiring special operating permits, etc.).

(f) Other, please specify (1) _____
_____ (most recent)
(2) _____
_____ (today)

Measure of Political Risk

5. Below are listed six methods for measuring political risk. Please check which method(s) your company (1) actually used at the time of investment to measure political risk for its most recent FDMI and (2) uses today to measure political risk for a typical potential FDMI.

	Most Recent FDMI	FDMI Today
(a)		
(b)		
(c)		
(d)		
(e)		
(f)		
(g)		

(a) Make subjective evaluation of political risk.

(b) Project a probability distribution of cash flows.

(c) Estimate the covariance of cash flows with other investment cash flows.

(d) Perform a sensitivity analysis.

(e) Calculate the probability of loss.

(f) Make no political risk assessment.

(g) Other, please specify (1) _____
_____ (most recent)
(2) _____
_____ (today)

Adjustment for Political Risk

6. Below are listed six adjustments that might be made in capital-budgeting procedures to account for political risk. Please check which method(s) your company (1) actually used at the time of investment to account for political risk in analyzing its most recent FDMI and (2) uses today in analyzing a typical potential FDMI.

	Most Recent FDMI	FDMI Today	
(a)			Vary rate of return required from the FDMI.
(b)			Vary cost of capital used in discounted cash flow analysis.
(c)			Vary payback period required from the FDMI.
(d)			Insure political risks and charge cash flows for cost of insurance.
(e)			Charge cash flows for cost of insuring political risks even if not taken.
(f)			Make no adjustment for political risk.
(g)			Other, please specify (1) _____ _____ (most recent) (2) _____ _____ (today)

Currency for Evaluating Foreign Investment

7. In making investment decisions, please check (✓) in which currency your company (1) evaluated its most recent FDMI and (2) evaluates a typical potential FDMI today.

	Most Recent FDMI	FDMI Today	
(a)			Dollars
(b)			Local currency
(c)			Both

Definition of Foreign Currency Risk

8. In analyzing a foreign investment, please check which definition(s) of exposure to foreign currency risk your company (1) used at the time of investment for analyzing its most recent FDMI and (2) uses today to analyze a typical potential FDMI.

	Most Recent FDMI	FDMI Today	
(a)			Accounting translation exposure (affiliate exposed assets--affiliate exposed liabilities according to FASB #8).
(b)			Accounting translation exposure plus affiliate transactions in foreign currencies.
(c)			Present cash flows to affiliate in foreign currencies.
(d)			Present and future cash flows to affiliate in foreign currency.
(e)			Present cash flows to parent in foreign currency.
(f)			Present and future cash flows to parent in foreign currency.
(g)			Other, please specify (1) _____ _____ (most recent) (2) _____ _____ (today)

Measure of Foreign Currency Risk

9. Below are listed six methods for measuring foreign currency risk. Please check (✓) which method(s) your company (1) used at the time of investment to measure foreign currency risk for its most recent FDMI and (2) uses today to measure foreign currency risk for a typical potential FDMI.

	Most Recent FDMI	FDMI Today	
(a)			Make subjective evaluation of foreign currency risk.
(b)			Project a probability distribution of cash flows.

	Most Recent FDMI	FDMI Today
(c)		
(d)		
(e)		
(f)		
(g)		

(c) Estimate covariance of cash flows with other investment cash flows.

(d) Perform a sensitivity analysis.

(e) Calculate the probability of loss.

(f) Make no foreign currency risk assessment.

(g) Other, please specify (1) _____
_____ (most recent)
(2) _____
_____ (today)

Adjustment for Foreign Currency Risk

10. Below are listed six adjustments that might be made in capital-budgeting procedures to account for foreign currency risk. Please check which method(s) your company (1) actually used at the time of investment to account for foreign currency risk in analyzing its most recent FDMI and (2) uses today in analyzing a typical potential FDMI.

	Most Recent FDMI	FDMI Today
(a)		
(b)		
(c)		
(d)		
(e)		
(f)		

(a) Vary rate of return required from the FDMI.

(b) Vary cost of capital used in discounted cash flow analysis.

(c) Vary payback period required from the FDMI.

(d) Insure foreign currency risks and charge cash flow for the cost.

(e) Charge cash flows for cost of insuring foreign currency risks even if not taken.

(f) Make no adjustment for foreign currency risk.

	Most Recent FDMI	FDMI Today
(g)		

Other, please specify (1) _____
_____ (most recent)
                      (2) _____
_____ (today)

Negative Impact of Foreign Risks

11. Below are listed several negative impacts that changes in the political or foreign currency environments could have on corporate earnings. Please check the geographic areas in which your company has sustained these effects at least once over the past 10 years.

Geographic Area

	Europe	Middle East	Africa	Asia & Far East	Latin America	Canada	Other
Accounting translation loss equal to at least 10% of an affiliate earnings							
Operating loss by affiliate due to currency change							
Operating loss of affiliate due to political change							
Shortfall of affiliate earnings by at least 10% from what would have occurred without currency change							
	(a)	(b)	(c)	(d)	(e)	(f)	(g)

Geographic Area

	Europe	Middle East	Africa	Asia & Far East	Latin America	Canada	Other
Shortfall of affiliate earnings by at least 10% from what would have occurred without political change							
	(a)	(b)	(c)	(d)	(e)	(f)	(g)

Section III: Company Information

Characteristics of Most Recent FDMI

1. Questions A to E ask for information <u>as of the time</u> of your company's <u>most recent foreign direct manufacturing investment</u> (FDMI). Please respond by placing a check (✓) in the proper box.

    A. In which geographic area was the investment made?

    Geographic Area

    (a) ☐ Europe   (e) ☐ Latin America

    (b) ☐ Middle East   (f) ☐ Canada

    (c) ☐ Africa   (g) ☐ Other, please specify

    (d) ☐ Asia and Far East   _____

    B. What was the primary activity of the affiliate at the time of investment?

	Industry	SIC Code
(a) ☐	Food Products	(20)
(b) ☐	Paper and Allied Products	(26)
(c) ☐	Chemicals and Allied Products	(28)
(d) ☐	Rubber Products	(30)

	Industry	SIC Code
(e) ☐	Primary and Fabricated Metals	(33, 34)
(f) ☐	Machinery (except electrical)	(35)
(g) ☐	Electrical Machinery	(36)
(h) ☐	Transportation Equipment	(37)
(i) ☐	Other, please specify _____	

C. What was the method of investment?

Method of Investment

(a) ☐ Acquire existing company   (b) ☐ Start new company

D. What was your company's share of ownership in the affiliate at the time of investment?

(a) ☐ 1 - 24%   (c) ☐ 51 - 99%

(b) ☐ 25 - 50%   (d) ☐ 100%

E. What was the approximate size of the investment? _____ million

Company Characteristics

2. Please check (✓) which of the following descriptions best characterizes the <u>worldwide organizational structure</u> of your company (1) at the time of your most recent FDMI and (2) today.

	Most Recent FDMI	Today	
(a)			Organized globally by geographic divisions.
(b)			Organized globally by functional area (e.g., finance, marketing, etc.).
(c)			Organized globally by product lines or groups.
(d)			Using international division for foreign operations.
(e)			Other, please describe (1) _____ _____ (most recent) (2) _____ _____ (today)

3. Based on your firm's results for the fiscal year of its most recent FDMI and the latest fiscal year, please complete the following information.

	Most Recent FDMI	Today	
(a)			Fiscal year
(b)	$	$	Gross sales for the total company (million $)
(c)	%	%	Percent of total gross sales from foreign operations
(d)	$	$	Total company assets (million $)
(e)	%	%	Percent of total assets in foreign operations
(f)	$	$	Total company net income after taxes (million $)
(g)	%	%	Percent of total net income after taxes from foreign operations

4. Please indicate below the number of countries in each area of the world where your company has a FDMI today.

	Number of Countries	
(a)		Europe
(b)		Middle East
(c)		Africa
(d)		Asia and Far East
(e)		Latin America
(f)		Canada
(g)		Other, please specify _____

5. Does your company have a potential FDMI under evaluation today?

   (a) [_____]   Yes

   (b) [_____]   No

Section IV: Comments

The questionnaire you have just completed was a structured approach to understanding foreign investment decision making in multinational companies. The questions in this section are designed to allow you the opportunity to comment.

1. Please check which of the following statements best describes the reason for differences between practices your company actually used to evaluate its most recent FDMI and those it uses today.

   (a) ☐ There are no differences.

   (b) ☐ Practices differ because of changes in standard company practices over time.

   (c) ☐ Practices differ because the country of the most recent FDMI required a unique analysis.

   (d) ☐ Practices differ because the activity of the most recent FDMI required a unique analysis.

   (e) ☐ Other, please specify _____

   Comments: _____
   _____
   _____

2. How do your company's practices today for evaluating foreign direct investments differ from those used today to analyze domestic investments? _____
   _____
   _____
   _____

3. Over the past 10 years, how have your company's methods of evaluating foreign investment opportunities changed? (Please give special attention in your response to changes, if any, in foreign currency risk and political risk definition and analysis.) _____

_____
_____
_____

4. In what areas, if any, would you like to see your company improve its foreign investment evaluation practices? _____

_____
_____
_____

5. In your opinion, what are the major obstacles that multinational companies face in trying to improve foreign investment decision making? _____

_____
_____
_____

6. Please indicate your name, title, and telephone number below so that I may contact you if I have any further questions.

   Name _____

   Title _____

   Telephone number (____) - _____
                     area
                     code

AGAIN, THANK YOU FOR YOUR SUPPORT OF THIS RESEARCH EFFORT.

Appendix C

Questions Covered in Field Survey

1. Please describe your role in your company's most recent FDMI decision.

2. Please describe briefly how a foreign investment decision is made including: who initiates a FDMI suggestion, to whom, what reports are required, and what information is requested.

3. In question 5, Section I, you ranked the financial criteria of investment. How, if at all, would this ranking change for a domestic investment? a foreign investment in another geographic area? in another industry?

4. Is the same cost of capital used for domestic and foreign investments? for all foreign investments?

5. Do you consider foreign investments "riskier" than domestic investment? Why? How is this accounted for in investment decisions?

6. Your company uses _____ to measure overseas business risk. Can you please explain how this measure is used? Why was the measure selected?

7. Your company adjusts for business risk by _____. Please explain. Why chosen?

8. Your company defines political risk in terms of _____. Does this vary by country? By type of operation?

9. Your company uses _____ to measure political risk. Please explain. Why chosen?

10. Your company adjusts for political risk by _____. Please explain. Why chosen?

11. Your company defines foreign currency risk in terms of _____. Please explain. Why chosen?

12. What impact has FASB #8 had on your company's investment evaluation methods?

13. Your company measures foreign currency risk by _____.
    Please explain. Why chosen?

14. Your company adjusts for foreign currency risks by _____.
    Please explain. Why chosen?

15. Question 11 in Section II indicates that your company has experienced losses due to foreign currency (political) risks. What, if any, changes have been made in your investment evaluation methods due to these losses?

16. Do you feel that environmental differences should be reflected in your firm's investment evaluation practices? Are they adequately?

17. What do you see as the major obstacles to improved corporate foreign investment analysis?

Notes

Chapter 1

1. This definition has been used in the *Survey of Current Business* statistics on foreign direct investment and also in the Harvard Multinational Enterprise Project.

2. Much of the definitional work in this section draws on Yair Aharoni's article, "On the Definition of a Multinational Corporation" (1971).

3. For other research on the balance-of-payments impact of foreign direct investment, see Lindert (1971), Stevens (1976), Caves (1974), and Adler and Stevens (1974).

4. This lack of consensus on the employment issue parallels the balance-of-payments controversy because the export displacement effect translates into lost domestic jobs.

Chapter 2

1. This same broad division is found in Ulrich Wesche (1974).

Chapter 3

1. This constant cost of capital is equal to the company-wide marginal cost of capital under the assumption that the subsidiary does not change the firm's frequency distribution of returns.

2. For a description of these indices see Green and Korth (1974).

3. Financial Accounting Standards Board Statement No. 8 outlines the procedures which accountants must follow in translating foreign currency transaction and subsidiary financial statements for inclusion in U.S. financial statements.

4. For other approaches to foreign currency exposure management, see Lietaer (1970), Shulman (1970), Wheelwright (1975), and Folks (1972).

Chapter 4

1. Cyert and March call this "dimensions of the goals" (1962, p. 115).

2. For tests of the behavioral theory of firm decision-making, see Clarkson (1962), Carter (1969), and Aharoni (1966).

Chapter 6

1. In 1978 these companies were required to report geographic financial breakout of Sales, Identifiable Assets, and Operating Income. Responses to the survey were crosschecked with corporate annual reports and the data adjusted to reflect these categories.

2. The matrix category includes companies responding to the questionnaire that marked the matrix category and also companies marking multiple categories, and so may overstate the usage of matrix organizations.

3. See Harrigan (1976), Morsicato (1978), Olstein and O'Glove (1973), Rodriquez (1974), and Teck (1974).

4. It should be noted at this point that some significant results occur by chance $1/20$ at $\alpha = .05$. Therefore, if many analyses are run on a single data set, the occurrence of some significant results may only be artifacts of the data and not represent true relationships.

5. This analysis was done between organizational structure today and evaluation practices today. It was not done on variables for most recent FDMI because of the high degree of correlation between practices at the two times.

Bibliography

Adler, M. "Framework for Research into Direct Manufacturing Investment Overseas." *Law and Contemporary Problems* 34 (1969), pp. 3-17.
_____. "The Valuation and Financing of the Multinational Firms: Comment." *Kyklos* 26 (1973), pp. 849-51.
_____. "Cost of Capital and a Two-Country Firm." *Journal of Finance* 29 (1974), pp. 119-32.
_____, and Dumas, B. "Optimal International Acquisitions." *Journal of Finance* 30 (1975), pp. 1-19.
_____, and Stevens, G.V. "The Trade Effects of Direct Investment." *Journal of Finance* 29 (1974), pp. 655-76.
Aggarwal, R. "Financial Policies for the MNC: The Management of Foreign Exchange," *Praeger Special Studies,* July 1976.
_____. "Theories of Foreign Direct Investment: A Summary of Recent Research and a Proposed Unifying Paradigm." *Economic Affairs* 22 (1977), pp. 31-45.
Aharoni, Y. *The Foreign Investment Decision Process.* Boston: Harvard University, 1966.
_____. "On the Definition of a Multinational Corporation." *Quarterly Review of Economics and Business* 11 (1971), pp. 27-37.
Aliber, R.Z. "A Theory of Direct Foreign Investment." In C.P. Kindleberger, ed., *The International Corporation.* Cambridge, Mass.: M.I.T. Press, 1970.
Arya, N.S. *Capital Budgeting in Multinational Firms: A Mathematical Approach.* Ph.D. dissertation, George Washington University, 1972.
Barnard, C.I. *The Functions of the Executive.* Cambridge, Mass.: Harvard University Press, 1956.
Barnet, R.J., and Müller, R.E. *Global Reach: The Power of the Multinational Corporations.* New York: Simon and Schuster, 1974.
Barnett, J.S. "Corporate Foreign Exposure Strategy Formulation." *Columbia Journal of World Business* 11 (1976), pp. 87-97.
Baumol, W.J. *Business Behavior, Value and Growth.* New York: The Macmillan Company, 1959.
Bavishi, V.B. "Capital Budgeting Study Among U.S. MNCs Indicates Current Practices/Trends." *Business International Money Report,* (June 8, 1979), pp. 194-95.
Behrman, J.N. *Direct Manufacturing Investment, Exports and the Balance of Payments.* New York: National Foreign Trade Council, 1968.
Bell, P.W. "Private Capital Movements and the U.S. Balance-of-Payments Position." In U.S. 87th Congress, Joint Economic Committee, Factors Affecting the U.S. Balance of Payments. Washington, D.C.: G.P.O., 1962, pp. 395-482.
Bennett, P.D., and Green, R.T. "Political Instability as a Determinant of Foreign Direct Investment in Marketing." *Journal of Marketing Research* 9 (1972), pp. 186-87.
Bergsten, C.F. "The Multinational Firms: Bane or Boom: Discussion." *Journal of Finance* 28 (1973), pp. 457-62.
_____, and Cline, W.R. "Increasing International Economic Interdependence: The Implications for Research." *American Economic Review* 66 (1976), pp. 155-61.

Boatwright, B.D., and Renton, G.A. "An Analysis of U.K. Inflows and Outflows of Direct Foreign Investment." *Review of Economics and Statistics* 57 (1975), pp. 478-86.

Boulding, K.E. *A Reconstruction of Economics.* New York: John Wiley & Sons, Inc., 1950.

Branson, W.H., and Hill, R.D. Jr. "Capital Movements Among Major O.E.C.D. Countries: Some Preliminary Results." *Journal of Finance* 26 (1971), pp. 269-86.

Brems, H. "A Growth Model of International Direct Investment." *American Economic Review* 60 (1970), pp. 320-31.

Bruck, N.K., and Lees, F.A. "Foreign Investment, Capital Controls and the Balance of Payments." *The Bulletin,* Institute of Finance, New York University, Graduate School of Business Administration, April 1968, No. 48-49.

Buckley, P.J., and Casson, M. *The Future of the Multinational Enterprise.* New York: Holmes & Neier Publishers, Inc., 1976.

Buckley, P.J., and Dunning, J.H. "The Industrial Structuring of U.S. Direct Investment in the U.K." *Journal of International Business Studies* 7 (1976), pp. 5-13.

Bugnion, J.R. "Capital Budgeting and International Corporations." In *International Finance for Multinational Business,* edited by Nehrt. Philadelphia, Pa.: Intext Educational Publishers, 1972.

Business International. *The Effects of U.S. Corporate Foreign Investment 1960-72.* 1974.

Carter, E.E. *A Behavioral Theory Approach to Firm Investment and Acquisition Decisions.* Ph.D. dissertation, Carnegie-Mellon University, 1969.

Caves, R.E. "International Corporations: The Industrial Economics of Foreign Investment." *Economica* 38 (1971), pp. 1-27.

──────. "Causes of Direct Investment: Foreign Firms' Shares in Canadian and U.K. Manufacturing Industries." *Review of Economics and Statistics* 56 (1974), pp. 279-93.

Clarkson, G.P.E. *Portfolio Selection: A Simulation of Trust Investment.* Englewood Cliffs, N.J.: Prentice-Hall, Inc., 1962.

──────, and Metzler, A.H. "Portfolio Selection: A Heuristic Approach." *Journal of Finance* 15 (1960).

──────, and Simon, H.A. "Microsimulation: The Simulation of Individual and Group Behavior." *American Economic Review,* 50 (1960).

Cohen, K.J. *Computer Models of the Shoe, Leather, Hide Sequence.* Englewood Cliffs, N.J.: Prentice-Hall, 1960.

──────, and Cyert, R.M. "Computer Models in Dynamic Economics." *Quarterly Journal of Economics* 75 (1961), pp. 112-27.

Committee on Finance, U.S. Senate. *Implications of Multinational Firms for World Trade and Investment and for U.S. Trade and Labor.* Washington, D.C.: U.S. Government Printing Office, February 1973.

Curhan, J.W., Davidson, H., and Luri, P. *Tracing the Multinationals: A Sourcebook.* Cambridge, Massachusetts: Ballinger Publishing Company, 1977.

Cutler, F., and Pizer, S. "U.S. Trade with Foreign Affiliates of U.S. Firms." *Survey of Current Business* 44 (1964), pp. 20-26.

Cyert, R.M., Dill, W.R., and March, J.G. "The Role of Expectations in Business Decision Making." *Administrative Science Quarterly* 31 (1958), pp. 307-40.

Cyert, R.M., Feigenbaum, E.A., and March, J.G. "Models in a Behavioral Theory of the Firm." *Behavioral Science* 4 (1959), pp. 81-95.

Cyert, R.M., and March, J.G. "A Behavioral Theory of Organizational Objectives." *Modern Organizational Theory,* ed. M. Haire. New York: Wiley, 1959.

──────. *The Behavioral Theory of the Firm.* Englewood Cliffs, N.J.: Prentice-Hall, Inc., 1962.

Cyert, R.M., Simon, H.A., and Trow, D.B. "Observation of a Business Decision." *The Journal of Business* 9 (1956), pp. 237-48.

Daniels, J.D. *Recent Foreign Direct Investment in the U.S.: An Interview Study of the Decision Process.* Ph.D. dissertation, University of Michigan, 1969.

_____, Ogram, E.W. Jr., and Radebaugh, L.H. *International Business: Environments and Operations.* Reading, Mass.: Addison-Wesley Publishing Co., 1976.

Davis, S.M. "Trends in the Organization of Multinational Corporations." *The Columbia Journal of World Business* 11, (1976), pp. 59-71.

Directory of American Firms Operating in Foreign Countries, 1979.

Dubin, M. *Foreign Acquisitions and the Spread of the Multinational Firm.* Ph.D. dissertation, Harvard University, 1976.

Dun and Bradstreet's *Million Dollar Directory,* 1977.

Dymsza, W.A. *Multinational Business Strategy.* New York: McGraw-Hill Book Co., 1972.

Eiteman, D.K., and Stonehill, A.I. *Multinational Business Finance.* Reading, Mass.: Addison-Wesley Publishing Co., 1973.

Fayerweather, J. *International Business Management: A Conceptual Framework.* New York: McGraw-Hill Book Co., 1969.

_____, and Kapoor, A. *Strategy and Negotiation for the International Corporation.* Cambridge, Mass.: Ballinger Publishing Co., 1976.

Fellner, W. *Competition Among the Few.* New York: Alfred A. Knopf, Inc., 1949.

Fisher, R.A. *Statistical Methods for Research Workers.* (9th ed.) London: Oliver and Boyd, 1954.

Folks, W.R., Jr. "Decision Analysis for Exchange Risk Management." *Financial Management* 1 (1972), pp. 101-12.

The Fortune Directory of the 500 Largest Industrial Corporations. 1977, 1978, 1979.

Gaddis, P.O. "Analyzing Overseas Investment." *Harvard Business Review* 44 (1966), pp. 115-22.

Gaston, J.F. "Direct Foreign Investment: Will Devaluation Hurt?" *Conference Board Record* 10 (1973), pp. 26-30.

Goldberg, M.A. "The Determinants of U.S. Direct Investment in the E.E.C.: Comment." *American Economic Review* 62 (1972), pp. 692-99.

Goldfinger, N. "A Labor View of Foreign Investment and Trade Issues." In *United States International Economic Policy in an Interdependent World: Paper I.* (Papers submitted to the Commission on International Trade and Investment, Washington, D.C., July 1971).

Gorecki, P.K. "The Determinants of Entry by Domestic and Foreign Enterprises in Canadian Manufacturing Industries: Some Comments and Empirical Results." *Review of Economics and Statistics* 58 (1976), pp. 485-88.

Gray, H.P., and Makinen, G.E. "The Balance of Payments Contributions of Multinational Corporations." *Journal of Business,* 40 (1967), pp. 339-43.

Green, R.T. *An Empirical Study of the Relationship Between Political Instability and Allocation and Flow of U.S. Foreign Direct Private Marketing Investment.* Ph.D. dissertation, The Pennsylvania State University, 1971.

_____, and Korth, C.M. "Political Instability and the Foreign Investor." *California Management Review* 17 (1974), pp. 23-31.

Grubel, H.G. *International Economics.* Homewood, Ill.: Richard D. Irwin, Inc., 1977.

Gull, D.S. "Composite Foreign Exchange Risk." *Columbia Journal of World Business* 10 (1975), pp. 51-69.

Haley, C.W., and Schall L.D. *The Theory of Financial Decisions.* New York: McGraw-Hill Book Co., 1973.

Harrigan, P. "The Double Sandbag in Foreign Exchange Accounting." *Euromoney* (June 1976), pp. 42-47.

Haskins, W.R. "How to Counter Expropriation." *Harvard Business Review* 48 (1970), pp. 102-12.

Hawkins, R.G. "U.S. Multinational Investment in Manufacturing and Domestic Economic Performance." Graduate School of Business Administration, New York University, Occasional Paper No. 1, February 1972.

_____, Mintz, N. and Provissiero, M. "Government Takeovers of U.S. Foreign Affiliates." *Journal of International Business Studies* (1976), pp. 3-16.

Bibliography

Haynes, E. "A Challenge to Critics of U.S. Foreign Investment." *Columbia Journal of World Business* 8 (1973), pp. 13-21.

Hays, W.L., and Winkler, R.L. *Statistics.* New York: Holt, Rinehart and Winston, Inc., 1971.

Heckerman, D. "The Exchange Risks of Foreign Operations." *Journal of Business* 45 (1972), pp. 422-48.

Hirsch, S. "An International Trade and Investment Theory of the Firm." *Oxford Economic Papers* 28 (1976), pp. 258-70.

Homans, G.C. *The Human Group.* New York: Harcourt, Brace and World, Inc., 1950.

Horst, T. "Firm and Industry Determinants of the Decision to Invest Abroad: An Empirical Study." *Review of Economics and Statistics* 54 (1972), pp. 258-66.

―――. "American Multinationals and the U.S. Economy," *American Economic Review* 66 (1976), pp. 149-54.

Hufbauer, G.C., and Adler, M. "Overseas Manufacturing Investment and the Balance of Payments." *U.S. Treasury Tax Policy Research Study No. 1.* Washington, D.C., 1968.

Hymer, S. *The International Operations of National Firms: A Study of Direct Investment.* Ph.D. dissertation, Cambridge, Mass.: M.I.T. Press, 1960.

―――. "The Efficiency (Contradictions) of the Multinational Corporations." *American Economic Review* 60 (1970), pp. 441-48.

―――. "The Internationalization of Capital." *Journal of Economic Issues* 6 (1972), pp. 91-111.

Imai, Y. "Exchange Rate Protection in International Business." *Journal of Financial and Quantitative Analysis* 10 (1975), pp. 447-56.

Johnson, H.G. "The Efficiency and Welfare Implications of the International Corporation." In *The International Corporation,* C.P. Kindleberger (ed.). Cambridge, Mass.: M.I.T. Press, 1970.

Jorgenson, D.W., and Siebert, C.D. "A Comparison of Alternative Theories of Corporate Investment Behavior." *American Economic Review* 18 (1968), pp. 681-712.

Jud, G.D. "The Multinational Expansion of U.S. Business: Some Evidence on Alternative Hypotheses." *Mississippi Valley Journal of Business and Economics* 10 (1975-1976), pp. 37-51.

Kapoor, A., and Grub, P.D. *The Multinational Enterprise in Transition.* Princeton, N.J.: The Darwin Press, 1973.

Katona, G. *Psychological Analysis of Economic Behavior.* New New: McGraw-Hill, 1951.

Katz, D. "Field Studies." *Research Methods in the Behavior Sciences,* ed. by L. Festinger and D. Katz. New York: The Dryden Press, 1953.

Keesee, D.G. "An Alternative to Hedging in Foreign Investments." *Management Accounting* 52 (1970), pp. 74-76.

Kelly, M. "Evaluating the Risk of Expropriation." *Risk Management,* 21 (1974), pp. 22-31.

Kerlinger, F.N. *Foundations of Behavioral Research.* New York: Holt, Rinehart and Winston, Inc., 1973.

Kim, S.H. "Financial Motives of U.S. Corporate Investment in Korea." *California Management Review,* 18 (1976), pp. 60-68.

Kindleberger, C.P. *American Business Abroad: Six Lectures on Direct Investment.* New Haven, Conn.: Yale University Press, 1969.

―――. *The International Corporation: A Symposium.* Cambridge, Mass.: The M.I.T. Press, 1970.

Klammer, T. "Empirical Evidence of the Adoption of Sophisticated Capital Budgeting Techniques." *Journal of Business* 45 (1972), pp. 387-97.

Knudson, T. "Explaining the National Propensity to Expropriate." *Journal of International Business Studies* 5 (1974), pp. 51-72.

Kobrin, S.J. "The Environmental Determinants of Foreign Direct Manufacturing Investment: An Ex-post Empirical Analysis." *Journal of International Business Studies* 7 (1976), pp. 29-42.

Kohlagen, S.W. "Exchange Rate, Changes, Profitability and Direct Foreign Investment," *Southern Economic Journal* 44 (1977), pp. 43-52.
Kopits, G.F. "Taxation and Multinational Firm Behavior: A Critical Survey." *International Monetary Fund Staff Papers* 23 (1976), pp. 624-73.
Kossack, E.W. *Initiating Motives for Foreign Direct Investment: The Georgia Carpet Industry.* Ph.D. dissertation, University of Georgia, 1977.
Kotowitz, Y., Sawyer, J.A., and Winder, W.L. *An Annual Econometric Model of the Canadian Economy, 1928-1966.* Toronto, Ontario: University of Toronto Press, 1968.
Krainer, R.F. "The Valuation and Financing of the Multinational Firm." *Kyklos* 25 (1972), pp. 553-74.
_____. "The Valuation and Financing of the Multinational Firm: Reply and Extensions." *Kyklos* 26 (1973), pp. 837-65.
Kwack, S.Y. *A Model for U.S. Direct Foreign Investment,* mimeographed. The Brookings Institution, Spring 1970.
Lall, S. "Transfer Pricing by Multinational Manufacturing Firms." *Oxford Bulletin of Economics and Statistics* 35 (1973), pp. 173-95.
_____. "LDC's and Private Foreign Direct Investment: A Review Article." *World Development* 2 (1974), pp. 43-48.
Laurence, M.M. and Severn, A.K. "Direct Investment, Research Intensity and Profitability." *Journal of Financial and Quantitative Analysis* 9 (1974), pp. 181-90.
Lecomber, R. "Overseas Investment: The Reddaway Report and Economic Theory." *Economic Journal* 81 (1971), pp. 588-92.
Lietaer, B.A. "Managing Risks in Foreign Exchange." *Harvard Business Review* 48 (1970), pp. 127-38.
Lilienthal, D.E. "Management and Corporations, 1985. New York: McGraw-Hill, 1960.
Lindert, P.H. "The Payments Impact of Foreign Investment Controls." *Journal of Finance,* 26 (1971), pp. 1083-100.
_____. "The Payments Impact of Foreign Investment Controls: Reply." *Journal of Finance* 31 (1976), pp. 1505-08.
Lloyd, B. "Political Risk Management." *Keith Shipton Developments Special Studies No. 7,* 1976.
Long, F. "Toward a Political Economy Framework of Foreign Direct Investment." *American Journal of Econ. Soc.* 36 (1977), pp. 171-85.
Long, N.V. "Expectation Revision and Optimal Learning in Foreign Investment Models." *International Economic Review* 17 (1976), pp. 247-61.
Makin, J.H. "The Portfolio Method of Managing Foreign Exchange Risk." *Euromoney* (August 1976), pp. 58-64.
Margolis, J. "Traditional and Revisionist Theories of the Firm." *Journal of Business* 32 (1959).
Mason, R.H. "Conflicts Between Host Countries and the Multinational Enterprise." *California Management Review* 17 (1974), pp. 5-14.
May, L.C. "Managing the Multinationals Exchange Risk." *Conference Board Record* 12 (1975), pp. 45-57.
McInnes, J.M. "Financial Control Systems for Multinational Operations: An Empirical Investigation." *Journal of International Business Studies* 2 (1971), pp. 11-28.
McKinnon, R.I. "International Firm and Efficient Economic Allocation: Discussion." *Economic Review* 60 (1970), pp. 451-53.
Merton, R.K. *Social Theory and Social Structure.* New York: The Free Press of Glencoe, Inc., 1957.
Moody's Industrial Manual, 1977, 1978, 1979.
Moose, J. *A Study of U.S. Direct Investment in Manufacturing and Petroleum Industries.* Ph.D. dissertation, Harvard University, 1968.

Morris, W.J., Jr. *Direct Foreign Investment and Public Policy: A Study of U.S. Postwar Experience.* Ph.D. dissertation, American University, 1968.

Morsicato, H. *An Investigation of the Interaction of Financial Statement Translation and Multinational Enterprise Performance Evaluation.* Ph.D. dissertation, The Pennsylvania State University, 1978.

The Multinational Corporation: Studies on U.S. Foreign Investment, Volume 1. Washington, D.C.: U.S. Department of Commerce, March 1972.

The Multinational Corporation: Studies on U.S. Foreign Investment, Volume 2. Washington, D.C.: U.S. Department of Commerce, April 1973.

Multinational Corporations in World Development. New York: United Nations, 1973.

National Foreign Trade Council, Inc. *The Impact of U.S. Foreign Direct Investment on U.S. Employment and Trade.* New York, 1971.

Naumann-Etienne, R. "A Framework for Financial Decisions in Multinational Corporations: Summary of Recent Research." *Journal of Financial and Quantitative Analysis* 9 (1974), pp. 859-74.

Nehrt, L.C. *International Finance for Multinational Business.* Scranton, Pa.: International Book Company, 1967.

Ness, W.R., Jr. "A Linear Programming Approach to Financing the Multinational Corporation." *Financial Management* 6 (1977), pp. 88-100.

Newell, A., and Simon, H.A. *Human Problem Solving.* Englewood Cliffs, N.J.: Prentice-Hall, Inc., 1972.

Noyes, G.E. "The Multinational Firm: Bane or Boom: Discussion." *Journal of Finance* 20 (1973), pp. 462-65.

Ohlin, B. *Interregional and International Trade.* Cambridge, Mass.: Harvard University Press, 1933 and 1967.

Olstein, R.A., and O'Glove, T.L. "Devaluation and Multinational Reporting." *Financial Analysts Journal* 29 (1973), pp. 65-84.

Papandreou, A. "Some Basic Problems in the Theory of the Firm." In *A Survey of Contemporary Economics,* ed. B.F. Haley. Homewood, Ill.: Richard D. Irwin, 1952.

_____. "The Multinational Firm: Bane or Boom: Discussion." *Journal of Finance* 28 (1973), pp. 455-57.

Penrose, E. "Foreign Investment and the Growth of the Firm." *Economic Journal* 66 (1956), pp. 220-36.

Piper, J.R., Jr. "How U.S. Firms Evaluate Foreign Investment Opportunities." *MSU Business Topics* 19 (1971), pp. 11-20.

Polk, J., Meister, I.S., and Veit, L.A. *U.S. Production Abroad and the Balance of Payments: A Survey of Corporate Investment Experience.* New York: National Industrial Conference Board, 1966.

Prachowrsy, M.F.J. *Direct Investment and the Balance of Payments: A Portfolio Approach,* mimeographed. The Brookings Institution, Spring 1970.

Quirin, G.D. *The Capital Expenditure Decision.* Homewood, Ill.: Richard D. Irwin, Inc., 1967.

Raggazi, G. "Theories of the Determinants of Direct Foreign Investment." *International Monetary Fund Staff Papers* 20 (1973), pp. 971-98.

Ray, E.J. "Foreign Direct Investment in Manufacturing." *Journal of Political Economy* 85 (1977), pp. 283-97.

Reddaway, W.B. *The Effect of U.K. Direct Investment Overseas: An Interim Report.* Cambridge, England: Cambridge University Press, 1967.

_____. *Effects of U.K. Direct Investment Overseas: Final Report.* Cambridge, England: Cambridge University Press, 1968.

Reder, M. "A Reconsideration of Marginal Productivity Theory." *Journal of Political Economy* 55 (1947), pp. 450-58.

Rhodes, J.B. "U.S. Investment Abroad: Who's Going Where, How and Why?" *Columbia Journal of World Business* 7 (1972), pp. 33-41.

Richardson, J.D. "On 'Going Abroad' the Firm's Initial Foreign Investment Decision." *Quarterly Review of Economics and Business* 11 (1971), pp. 7-21. (a)

_____. "Theoretical Considerations in the Analysis of Foreign Direct Investment." *Western Economic Journal* 9 (1971), pp. 87-98. (b)

Robbins, S.M. "Nine Investments Abroad and Their Impact at Home." *Columbia Journal of World Business* 11 (1976), pp. 111-14.

_____, and Stobaugh, R.B. "Bent Measuring Stick for Foreign Subsidiaries." *Harvard Business Review* 51 (1973), pp. 80-88. (a)

_____, and Stobaugh, R.B. *Money in the Multinational Enterprise.* New York: Basic Books, Inc., 1973. (b)

Robinson R.D. *International Business Management: A Guide to Decision Making.* Hinsdale, Ill.: Dryden Press, 1973.

Robock, S.H. "International Firm and Efficient Economic Allocation." *American Economic Review* 60 (1970), pp. 450-51.

_____. "Political Risk Identification and Assessment." *Columbia Journal of World Business* 6 (1971), pp. 6-20.

_____, Simmonds, K., and Zwick, R. *International Business and Multinational Enterprises.* Homewood, Ill.: Richard D. Irwin, Inc., 1973 and 1977.

Rodriquez, R.M. "Management of Foreign Exchange Risk in U.S. Multinationals." *Journal of Financial and Quantitative Analysis* 9 (1974), pp. 849-57.

_____, and Carter, E.E. *International Financial Management.* Englewood Cliffs, N.J.: Prentice-Hall, Inc., 1976.

Root, F.R. "U.S. Business Abroad and Political Risks." *MSU Business Topics* 16 (1968), pp. 73-80.

Rugman, A.M. "Corporate International Diversification and Market Assigned Measures of Risk and Diversification: A Discussion." *Journal of Financial and Quantitative Analysis* 10 (1975), pp. 651-52.

Rummel, R.J., and Heenan, D.A. "How Multinationals Analyze Political Risk." *Harvard Business Review* 56 (1978), pp. 67-76.

Safarian, A.E. "Perspectives on Foreign Direct Investment from the Viewpoint of a Capital Receiving Country." *Journal of Finance* 28 (1973), pp. 419-38.

Scaperlanda, A.F., and Mauer, L.J. "The Determinants of U.S. Direct Investment in the E.E.C." *American Economic Review* 59 (1969), pp. 558-68.

_____. "The Determinants of U.S. Direct Investment in the E.E.C.: Reply." *American Economic Review* 62 (1972), pp. 700-04.

Schall, L.D., Lunden, G.L., and Geijsbeek, W.R., Jr. "Survey and Analysis of Capital Budgeting Methods." *The Journal of Finance* (1978), pp. 281-87.

Schilling, D. "Devaluation Risk and Forward Exchange Theory." *American Economic Review* 60 (1970), pp. 721-27.

Schwartz, R.H. *The Determinants of U.S. Direct Investment Abroad.* Ph.D. dissertation, Texas Technological University, 1976.

Scitovsky, T. "A Note on Profit Maximization and Its Implications." *The Review of Economic Studies* 11 (1943), pp. 57-60.

Servan-Schreiber, J.J. *The American challenge.* London: Hamish Hamilton, 1968.

Sethi, S.P., and Holton, R.H. "Country Typologies for the Multinational Corporation: A New Basic Approach." *California Management Review* 15 (1973), pp. 105-18.

Severn, A.K. *Short Run Investment and Financial Behavior of U.S. Direct Investors in Manufacturing.* Ph.D. dissertation, University of Pennsylvania, September 1971.

_____. "The Valuation and Financing of the Multinational Firm: Comment." *Kyklos*, 26 (1973), pp. 852-56.

Bibliography

———. "Investor Evaluation of Foreign and Domestic Risk." *Journal of Finance* 29 (1974), pp. 545-50.

Shapiro, A.C. "Exchange Rate Changes, Inflation and the Value of the Multinational Corporation." *Journal of Finance* 30 (1975), pp. 485-502.

———. "Defining Exchange Risk." *Journal of Business* 50 (1977), pp. 37-39.

———, Rutenberg, D.P. "When to Hedge Against Devaluation." *Management Science* 20 (1974), pp. 1514-30.

———, and Rutenberg, D.P. "Managing Exchange Risks in a Floating World." *Financial Management* 5 (1976), pp. 48-58.

Shulman, R.B. "Are Exchange Risks Measurable?" *Columbia Journal of World Business* 5 (1970), pp. 55-60.

Simon, H.A. *Administrative Behavior*. New York: Macmillan, 1947.

———. "A Behavioral Model of Rational Choice." *Quarterly Journal of Economics* 69 (1952), pp. 99-118.

Smith, C.N. "Predicting the Political Environment of International Business." *Long Range Planning* 4 (1971), pp. 7-14.

Snyder, L. "Have Accountants Really Hurt the Multinationals?" *Fortune* 95 (1977), pp. 85-89.

Special Survey of U.S. Multinational Companies, 1970. Washington, D.C.: U.S. Department of Commerce, 1972.

Standard and Poor's Corporation Records, 1977, 1978, 1979.

Standard and Poor's Register of Corporations, Directors and Executives, 1979.

Stevens, G.V.G. "The Payments Impact of Foreign Investment Control: Comment." *Journal of Finance* 31 (1976), pp. 362-66.

Stobaugh, R.B., Jr. "How to Analyze Foreign Investment Climate." *Harvard Business Review* 47 (1969), pp. 100-08. (a)

———. "Where in the World Should We Put That Plant?" *Harvard Business Review* 47 (1969), pp. 129-36. (b)

Stonehill, A.I. *Readings in International Financial Management*. Pacific Palisades, Calif.: Goodyear Publishing Co., Inc., 1970.

———, and Nathanson, L. "Capital Budgeting and the Multinational Corporation." *California Management Review* 10 (1968), pp. 39-54.

Survey of Current Business. Washington, D.C.: Bureau of Economic Analysis, U.S. Department of Commerce, 1976.

Teck, A. "Control Your Exposure to Foreign Exchange." *Harvard Business Review* 52 (1974), pp. 66-75.

Tiffany, K.C. "Decisive Factors in the Decision to Invest in One Country Rather than Another." *Canadian Chartered Accountant* 96 (1968), pp. 188-92.

Treuherz, R.M. "Re-evaluating ROI for Foreign Operations." *Financial Executive* 36 (1968), pp. 64-71.

Truitt, J.F. *Expropriation of Private Foreign Investment: A Framework to Consider the Post World War II Experience of British and American Investors*. Ph.D. dissertation, Indiana University, 1970.

U.S. Direct Investments Abroad. Part I: Balance of Payments Data. Washington, D.C.: U.S. Department of Commerce, 1966.

Vaistos, C.V. *Interaffiliate Charges by Transnational Corporations and Intercountry Income Distribution*. Ph.D. dissertation, Harvard University, 1972.

Vernon, R. "International Investment and International Trade in the Product Cycle." *Quarterly Journal of Economics* 80 (1966), pp. 190-207.

———. *Manager in the International Economy*. Englewood Cliffs, N.J.: Prentice-Hall, Inc., 1968.

_____. *Sovereignty at Bay: The Multinational Spread of U.S. Enterprises.* New York: Basic Books, Inc., 1971.

_____. *The Economic and Political Consequences of Multinational Enterprises: An Anthology.* Boston: Harvard University, Graduate School of Business Administration, Division of Research, 1972.

_____. "U.S. Direct Investment in Canada Consequences for the U.S. Economy." *Journal of Finance* 28 (1973), pp. 407-17.

_____. "The Economic Consequences of U.S. Foreign Direct Investment." In *International Trade and Finance: Readings,* ed. by R.E. Baldwin and J.D. Richardson. Boston: Little, Brown and Co., 1974.

_____. "Storm Over the Multinational: Problems and Prospects." *Foreign Affairs* 55 (1977), pp. 243-62.

Villonueva, R.T. "The Case For and Against the Multinationals." *Conference Board Record* 10 (1973), p. 61.

Walia, T.S. *An Empirical Evaluation of Selected Theories of Foreign Direct Investment by U.S. Based Multinational Corporations.* Ph.D. dissertation, New York University, 1976.

Weber, M. *The Theory of Social and Economic Organization.* New York and London: Oxford University Press, 1947.

Wesche, U. *Major Theories of Direct Private Investment and the Experience of German Multinational Manufacturing Enterprises.* Ph.D. dissertation, 1974.

Weston, J.F., and Sorge, B.W. *International Managerial Finance.* Homewood, Ill.: Richard D. Irwin, Inc., 1972.

Wheelwright, S.C. "Applying Decision Theory to Improve Corporate Management of Currency Exchange Risks." *California Management Review* 17 (1975), pp. 41-49.

Willett, T.D. "International Firms and Efficient Economic Allcoation: Discussion." *American Economic Review* 60 (1970), pp. 449-50.

Williamson, O.E. "Managerial Discretion and Business Behavior." *American Economic Review* 53 (1963), pp. 1032-57.

Woodbury, J.R., III. *Foreign Investment: A Synthesis of Organization, Trade and Capital Theoretic Approaches.* Ph.D. dissertation, Washington University, 1977.

Zenoff, D.B., and Zwick, J. *International Financial Management.* Englewood Cliffs, N.J.: Prentice-Hall, Inc., 1969.

Zwick, J. "Models for Multicountry Investments." *Business Horizons* 10 (1967), pp. 69-74.

Index

abilities and competitive advantage, 17, 19, 20, 21
Adler, 8, 10, 11, 177
aggressive motives, 75
Aharoni, 5, 34, 39, 41-43, 46, 59, 61, 132, 152, 160, 162, 167-69, 173-74, 176
Aliber, 17, 18, 21, 25
allowance for risk, 28, 29, 30
Alman, 24

balance of payments, 8, 10-11, 13-14, 17
Banks and Textor Measure, 31
Barnard, 35-36
Barnet, 8-9
Baumol, 35
Bavishi, 30, 62, 153, 162-65, 172
behavioral theory, 6, 28, 34-39, 42, 44, 48, 50, 55, 59, 60-64, 73, 80, 130, 132-33, 139, 140, 143-44, 152, 159-60, 166-67, 169, 172-74, 176
Behnman, 8, 11, 12
Bell, 10
Boatwright, 24
Boulding, 35
Bugnion, 29
Business International, 13, 45
business risk, 86, 89, 91, 103, 107, 119, 123, 125, 128, 133, 135, 139, 147, 154-57, 160, 164-65

capital budgeting, 29-30, 49, 59, 68, 89, 91, 95-96, 101, 113, 159-160, 165-66, 169, 176
capital intensity under differential income valuation, 17, 21
Carter, 29, 46, 83, 133, 166, 167, 174
cash flow, 28-30, 33, 86, 89, 91, 95, 100, 113, 118, 123, 125, 154, 156, 170
Caves, 22-23, 25, 117
Clarkson, 46, 61, 160
Cohen, 46
competition, 9
cost of capital, 28-30, 60, 73, 83, 86-87, 89, 101, 103, 107, 110, 113, 115, 119, 123, 125, 130, 147, 154, 159-60, 163, 166, 170-71
Curhan, 44
currency risk, 28-29, 33-34, 49, 55, 64, 71, 87, 89, 91, 96, 100, 103, 107, 113, 118, 123, 125, 130, 133, 135, 139, 140, 147, 154, 156-57, 159-60, 164-65, 170, 172, 175
Cutler, 45
Cyert, 35-39, 46, 61-62, 80, 166-69, 174, 176

Daniels, 5
Davidson, 44
Davis, 61
DCF. *See* discounted cash flow
defensive motives, 75
differential interest rates, 17, 18, 25
discounted cash flow, 28, 30, 34, 60, 80, 89, 100, 156, 162-65, 169-70
Dubin, 43
Dymsza, 28-29

economic impact, 7-10, 17, 159
economic, imperialism, 10
employment, 10, 114, 17
exchange risk. *See* currency risk
exploratory field research, 46-48, 55, 169
export displacement, 10-11
ex post facto research, 44-45, 47

Feierabend Index, 31
Fellner, 35
foreign currency. *See* currency risk

Gaddis, 29
Goldberg, 23
Goldfinger, 13
go-no go analysis, 37, 78, 161-62, 174
Green, 31
growth of the firm, 17, 18, 25
Gull, 33

Haner Index, 31
Harrigan, 33
Harvard Multinational Enterprise Project, 6, 20, 43-44, 59, 169-70
Hawkins, 7-8, 14

Index

Homans, 35
Horst, 8, 14, 23, 117
Hufbauer, 8, 10-11, 177
Hymer, 9, 16, 18-23, 25, 42

indirect benefits, 30
internal rate of return, 29-30, 80, 83, 144, 162, 165, 169
IRR. *See* internal rate of return

Katy, 45-46, 48, 59, 169
Kerlinger, 44-45, 47-48
Kim, 34, 45
Kindleberger, 19
Klammer, 45, 68, 153, 165, 166
Korth, 31
Kotowitz, 18
Kwack, 18

Labor, 7, 11, 13
Lilienthal, 5
loss history, 139-40
Luri, 44

management superiority, 17, 22
March, 35-39, 46, 61-62, 80, 166, 168-69, 174, 176
Margolis, 36
Mauer, 23
McInnes, 54, 68
Meister, 17, 18
Merton, 36
Moose, 18
Morsicato, 45, 68, 170-71

Nathanson, 28-29, 42, 45, 68, 86, 162-64
National Industrial Conference Board, 18
normative theories, 27-30, 80, 83, 86-87, 100, 159, 164, 176-78

Ogram, 5
Ohlin, 16
organizational theory, 131-32

Pascal, 24
payback, 80, 83, 89, 95, 100, 135, 153-54, 162-66
Piper, 27, 34, 162, 164
Pizer, 45
political risk, 28-31, 34, 49, 55, 62, 71, 80, 87, 89, 91, 95-96, 100, 103, 107, 110, 113, 115, 119, 123, 125, 130, 133, 135, 139-40, 147, 153-56, 159-60, 164-65, 170, 172, 175
Polk, 17, 18, 73, 161-63
positive analysis, 159
positive theories, 15-16, 18-22, 24-25, 27, 34, 159, 177. *See also* differential interest rates; growth of the firm; abilities and competitive advantage; R & D capability in the product life cycle; capital intensity under differential income valuation; management superiority
Prachowrsy, 18
product differentiation, 22

R & D capability in the product life cycle, 17, 20
Radebaugh, 5
Ray, 24
Reder, 35
Renton, 24
return on investment, 80, 89, 104, 107
Richardson, 34
risk rating, 50, 55, 59-64, 71, 87, 89, 100, 133, 155, 156, 162, 171, 175, 178
Robbins, 6, 43, 59, 62, 103, 107, 109, 169
Robock, 30-31
Rodriguez, 29, 83
Russet Measure, 31
Rutenberg, 33

Sawyer, 18
Scaperlanda, 23
Scholl, 45, 68, 153, 165, 166
Scitovsky, 35
Sexvan and Schreiber, 16, 18, 22, 25
Shapiro, 33
Simon, 35-37, 46
Snyder, 33
Sorge, 83
Stevens, 8
Stobaugh, 6, 29, 37, 43, 59, 62, 103, 107, 109, 169
Stonehill, 28-29, 42, 45, 68, 162-64

taxation, 9
technology, 8-9
Teck, 33

U.S. Department of Commerce, 44-45

Vaistos, 8
Veit, 17, 18
Vernon, 5-6, 8, 17, 20-21, 23, 25, 42-43

Weber, 36
Wesche, 24
Weston, 83
Williamson, 35

Zenoff, 28-29
Zwick, 28-29